C000171069

Lincolnshire
MURDERS

Lincolnshire
MURDERS

Stephen Wade

The
History
Press

First published in 2006 by Sutton Publishing Limited

Reprinted in 2009 by
The History Press
The Mill, Brimscombe Port,
Stroud, Gloucestershire, GL5 2QG
www.thehistorypress

Reprinted 2011

Copyright © Stephen Wade, 2011

All rights reserved. No part of this publication may be reproduced, stored in
a retrieval system, or transmitted, in any form or by any means, electronic,
mechanical, photocopying, recording or otherwise, without the prior permission of
the publisher and copyright holder.

Stephen Wade has asserted the moral right to be identified as the author of this work.

British Library Cataloguing in Publication Data
A catalogue record for this book is available from the British Library.

ISBN 978-0-7509-4321-5

Typeset in 10.5/13.5pt Sabon.
Typesetting and origination by
Sutton Publishing Limited.
Printed and bound in Great Britain by
Marston Book Services Limited, Didcot

CONTENTS

ACKNOWLEDGEMENTS

The author is indebted to and would like to thank the staff of the Lincolnshire Archives and Lincoln City Libraries, who were a great help. Also particular thanks are due to retired police officers Charles Watkinson, John Olsson and Mick Alcock of the Lincolnshire forces, and to A.A. Clarke who did pioneering work on some cases. Researchers and writers of the Police History Society provided some little-known information to add to the standard material. Locally, Chris Horan at the *Scunthorpe Evening Telegraph* has to be thanked for help with an appeal for information, as has Stephen Hill, formerly of Brigg. There has also been support from the Society for Lincolnshire History and Archaeology.

Picture material, when not in the author's collection, is from the Lincolnshire County Council Collections. The original drawings were created by Laura Carter. Rosalind Boyce was a very helpful researcher for the Lincoln pictorial references, and Jackie Cole and Chris Horan with the 1945 Scunthorpe story.

PICTURE CREDITS

The pictures, where indicated, are from the Local Studies Collection, Lincoln Central Library and Lincolnshire Archives, by courtesy of Lincolnshire County Council, Education and Cultural Services Directorate. The unpublished memoirs of Constable Harry Johnson were also invaluable.

INTRODUCTION

Lincolnshire has an undeserved reputation for blandness. The popular view of it as a flat county, almost entirely given over to agriculture, is easily caught on a fleeting visit. But this opinion is as false as the common statements made about its history. Because of its urban character, the county is not comparable to West Yorkshire or the Midland conurbations, but it is not the case that Lincolnshire has not seen war, civil strife or horrific crimes.

On the surface Lincoln appears to be only a typical tourist destination, mainly interesting because of its distant medieval past. In fact, it has been the site of vicious riots, notorious murders and revolts of felons of all kinds, and has long been a city of prisons, gaols and lock-ups. Not only does it have a castle prison, a dour Victorian edifice, but also a prison on Greetwell Road, in the celebrated Victorian Gothic style, after several London models. Even in the city centre, as visitors pass under the arches of the Stonebow, they are walking past a former gaol whose desperate inhabitants would beg from the cellar windows for drinks or coins.

It is also the county of convicts, who were shipped to Australia and Van Dieman's Land in massive numbers: between 1788 and 1840 over 110,000 were transported. Some of them, such as William Laughton of Coningsby, were transported for life just for stealing things like cotton and silk garments. Only one of the killers described in this book was sentenced to that fate, and it seems that he drowned early in the journey.

The county stretches from the Humber estuary down to the Wash, and therefore the settings of the murder cases in this book are anything from a misty fenland to an industrial town, or from a farmhouse to a noisy rural inn. These cases deal with some of the main murders in the county from the Regency period to the 1960s; three are unsolved murders and one is entirely political, with no known suspects. Most of the stories have been told before, and some of those are described briefly only. I have been able to flesh out the more recent cases with a range of sources from professionals involved in the police work, or from people who have ancestors located around the cases. Only one case, the notorious Tom Otter, has attained the status of local myth.

Lincolnshire has been stereotyped as a county linked to poaching, as in the famous song of 'The Lincolnshire Poacher'. But there is much more to the history of crime there, as I hope that these accounts of murders both domestic and communal will illustrate. Unlike many British cities, Lincoln has never been home to a huge underclass of immigrants and paupers, and offers different and enlightening off-shoots from social history, which I hope will not disappoint the reader.

The study of true crime and the history of violent crime against the person is merely another way of understanding how people lived, and how they lived together. Sometimes they had led vulnerable lives, subject to many risks; sometimes they simply cracked under the strain of hard work and family or financial pressures. Thus it is significant that when the new asylum for the mentally ill was opened at Bracebridge in Lincoln, in the last years of the Victorian period, it catered for almost a thousand people. Over a century before, the county produced the family of doctors who cured George III's mental illness (some historians now believe his illness was porphyria).

Many of the homicide cases recorded in the Lincolnshire Assizes archive lack detail; some potentially fascinating cases have no substantial narrative for this reason. I have also omitted some eighteenth-century cases for similar reasons, but one in particular was so fascinating that it is included in the miscellany of shorter pieces at the end of the book. The best printed secondary source for these pre-1800 murders is B.J. Davey's book, *Rural Crime in the Eighteenth Century*, and he lists only six cases between 1770 and 1800, all of which have only minimal sources with very little detail available.

Though my main sources for the principal cases of the nineteenth century have been in secondary narratives, an element of oral and community history has been interwoven in the retelling of the last three. For the very early stories, the recently refurbished museum and documents archive at Lincoln Castle have been a useful source, as has the labour of love undertaken by Paul R.L. Williams and his CD reference work on police murders, *The Ultimate Price*. For the established narratives of the more celebrated cases, I have to thank the writer Adrian Gray, whose two books on this area of history have been very helpful, and John Olsson for the interview about the Stephenson case.

The contrasts between town and country in the county's crime have been marked, and such subjects as the development of the police force after the 1857 new jurisdictions involved a number of major problems, as the case from Hemingby shows. Otherwise, the narratives interwoven with these murder tales are often about professionals who were present but not prominent, such as chief constables or administrators. The main contexts of homicide in Lincolnshire enmesh the historian in all kinds of microhistory, which are the product of local historians who have delved into records in obscure parishes, and these have shown me that one of the rewards of researching crime history is the delight of serendipity.

I have included a liberal sprinkling of anecdotal and fragmentary material, much of which relates to prominent murder cases, but which perhaps deserves separate treatment. A typical example is the kind of memoir reaching back to the Victorian period, such as a tale told by a woman in 1960 who had interviewed a man thirty years before. He had been present at the last public hanging: he was one of a crowd of 20,000 who saw the killers Carey and Picket hanged at Cobb Hall. Where possible, I have incorporated this kind of material.

But the intention has been to interweave narratives of human frailties and mistakes, passions and emotions, plans and projects, which in one way or another illuminate the larger picture of social change in Lincolnshire. In some ways, where the county lagged behind other parts of England in economic or social terms, tradition and neglect came together to make its people less aware of the changing world of more advanced technology and communication that was Victorian society. This helps us understand such cases as the Biggadike and Lefley murders.

Other cases are entirely typical of the social context of their time. The historical factors are usually plain to see; the legal questions are invariably complex and at times insoluble. Most of the trials here involve moral complexities which all the professionals at work in court found challenging in the extreme.

1

TOM OTTER GIBBETED

Saxilby, 1805

The surname Otter was very common across Lincolnshire up to the 1840s. In 1846, for instance, John Otter was Lord of the Manor in Kirton and there was a large family of that name in the area, and it is still common around Lincoln. But Otter is a name in the annals of Lincolnshire crime with a special and haunting resonance, as this story shows.

The village of Saxilby, a small, isolated place in the early nineteenth century, was difficult to find if you left the main roads. It is situated between Lincoln and Gainsborough, close to Doddington Hall, a stately home. At the time of this murder it was in the heart of the farmland below the long ridge running from the north of the county down to the south of Lincoln to the River Witham. Even today the string of villages dotted along the rich green land between north Nottinghamshire and Lindsey are often hardly noticed by travellers if they miss the main roads. There is a steep incline in parts from the Burton road north of Lincoln, and this continues all the way north to Kirton.

With this in mind, it is not difficult to see how a dangerous man like Otter might think he could brutally murder his new wife and hide her body in a lonely place. But he was wrong.

The story begins with a setting almost comparable to that of one of Thomas Hardy's tragic novels, and the rural context is very much of that world of masters and men, poor servants, tough labourers and relentless, confident authority. Otter, or Temporal as he was also known, was one of that class of casual labourers who inhabit the darker areas of employment history, in an era when hired labour often came from the hiring fairs, where men would count on their appearance as well as their track record to secure a new post. We might now refer to Otter as marginalised. He appears to have worked in order to secure enough money for drink, and only thought about more work when it was exhausted. In this case, the focus of the story is the Sun Inn in Saxilby, where he sometimes did his drinking.

The killer was one of the so-called bankers, a wild breed of men who did the toughest work in the maintenance of the irrigation systems in the fields, and when there were urgent problems as the result of silting. Bankers were notoriously rough characters, and memoirs written late in the nineteenth century relate tales of the lawlessness of this occupation.

Otter/Temporal's family came from Treswell, near Retford. His father, Thomas, married Ann Temporal on 30 July 1775. Ann was forty-five, unusually late for marriage at that time. It was a 'shotgun wedding' it seems, as Ann gave birth to a daughter just a few weeks after the marriage. Tom Otter, the future murderer, was the third child in the family, being born when his mother was fifty-one, in 1782. The boy was only sixteen when his father died, and he was brought up by an uncle. He seems to have had a nasty personality and a very cruel streak, as some accounts testify to his cutting animals for pleasure.

By 1805 Otter had gained a reputation as a wandering scoundrel; he most likely had more than one love affair in progress at any time, but on this occasion one Mary Kirkham was with child by him and he would be coerced into marrying her. It was most important for pregnant women to marry at this time. There was a high incidence of suicide and infanticide. 'Shamed' young women were regularly reported as suicide cases in such journals as the *Gentleman's Magazine*, as in this report from 1806: 'Elizabeth Trout, a young woman, of Little Sheffield, who in a fit of despair, drowned herself in a pond, which being frozen over, she broke a hole in the ice, just to admit her head, which she put into the water, while the whole of her body remained quite dry. . . .' Again, only twenty years later, in Louth, a young woman who had been 'seduced' by a 'local religious gentleman' killed her child and was found out. She killed herself in Lincoln Castle while awaiting trial.

Tom Temporal, however, already had a wife and child in Southwell. He used a false name in this new bigamous marriage, his mother's maiden name. Given the small communities involved here, and the state of communications at the time, it seems unlikely that anyone back home in Nottinghamshire would have found out about the unlawful union in this tiny village, off the beaten track, and it was well away from Lincoln itself, where there might have been a slight possibility of his being recognised by travellers.

The marriage took place at South Hykeham, only a few miles from Saxilby. Two local officers, called Shuttleworth, stood beside the groom during the swift and perfunctory service. Otter was taken there by the constables with the charge of bastardy on him, in a cart to be sure he actually arrived. It is useful at this point to recall that in the late eighteenth century illegitimacy was regulated, where possible, by bastardy bonds. A pregnant single woman was perceived as an offence against her local community. Overseers and churchwardens needed to know how the child would be supported and educated, of course. A girl who said nothing about the father when standing before magistrates for this summary offence would be taken to a house of correction. But when the father was identified, a bastardy bond was made, demanding his payment of £40 over a set period, to pay for everything from the midwife's fees to general maintenance. These factors explain why Otter was taken in hand in Hykeham on this occasion.

In the register there are simply marks made by both people. The newly-weds then set off for Lincoln, where Otter was labouring in the old swan-pool. He had first met Mary in the city while he was banking at the pool. It was 6 p.m. by the time they reached Saxilby.

It was not uncommon for young men like Otter to be marched to the altar, but he resented it deeply and the rancorous emotion gnawed at him, insisting on some kind of wild vengeance. Otter wasted no time in planning his wife's death and finding a suitable place for it. He took her for a walk from the Sun Inn in Saxilby to a place called Drinsey Nook. Unluckily for him, another labourer also took a walk that way, possibly as a 'peeping Tom', but also to continue a journey towards the village of Harby. This was John Dunkerly, and he made a long and detailed statement about what he saw, though only after the trial had taken place. The couple walked to a quiet spot, and then, as Dunkerly reported, Otter said to Mary, 'Sit down, you can rest here.' He then he walked into the undergrowth and took a hedge-stake. According to Dunkerly, 'The moon shined on his face at the time and his eyes frightened me, there was such a fiery look in them, like a cat's eyes in the dark. And I heard him say to himself, "That'll finish my . . . wedding!" Then he climbed down to where she was sitting with her head hanging down, and he swung the hedge-stake with both hands and hit her a clout on the head.'

Two other men had witnessed Mary and Otter walk to the Nook. Dunkerly had also walked past them. They knew him, as he worked on local land, and they said to him, 'You'll have company, John.'

It appears that Dunkerly was very close, though well camouflaged as he watched events unfold. His account of the murder and the body is convincing; it is also graphic in detail. He noted that Mary's body was 'all a-quiver like' before she became rigid. He described the second blow as like hitting a turnip. He said that he passed out, and that when he came round 'the hedge-stake Otter had murdered her with lay close beside me'.

Dunkerly suffered a serious trauma from witnessing such a terrible crime. He recounts how he touched the stake and got blood on his hands and smock and then he wandered aimlessly around the area for days: 'I wandered about, I don't know how long, working on the roads and getting a job as how I could . . . I come back to Doddington on the twentieth of March.'

There are some difficulties with the dating of events in this case. The Otter marriage took place on 3 November 1805. The arrest must have taken place after the body was found, and that was apparently before Dunkerly surfaced. The date of Otter's trial was technically on 8 March 1808, as that was the set

The Strugglers Inn, where the condemned prisoner would take a last drink. (Author's Collection)

date for the circuit judges to attend the Lincoln and City Assize, according to the records, but other sources give the 12th as the date.

Mary's body was found by Thomas Bowker and Daniel Fletcher, and the inquest was set in motion, while Dunkerly wandered away, most disturbed and apprehensive. He was away for a long time and only reappears in the story much later, well after the key events in the process of arrest and trial. Reading between the lines of his story, he was naturally very afraid of being accused of the murder; he had had Mary Kirkham's blood on him for the rest of the day in question, and he must have needed to find a way to wash his smock without being questioned. Obviously there were no subtleties of forensic enquiry then, but he must have panicked.

On the day of the murder he had walked a long way to the Sun Inn, then drunk for some considerable time, no doubt talking about Lord Nelson and Trafalgar, the big news of only two weeks before. Then he had to walk a long way, north of Drinsey Nook towards the village of Harby, a walk of several miles.

The body was found and Otter arrested, and an inquest held. The incidents that accompanied the arrest and inquest are disturbing and unpleasant. For instance, one account, written fifty years ago, notes that he was arrested in the inn, and that this was fitting: 'Its sign was the sun, and it was in the sunshine he was caught. He was sitting by the window, in a shaft of winter sunlight, and the sunlight fell upon a portion of his coat and threw up a multi-coloured sheen . . . and this sheen was so marked that it held the eye of a rural constable who had had enough experience of farmyards to recognise that sheen.'

Also, when Kirkham's body was brought to the inn for the inquest, it was reported that blood spilled from the body on to the wooden planks of the cart and dripped from underneath it. Naturally there would have been no blood in liquid form to spill at that point. Nevertheless, it gave rise to legends about the Otter case. In 1930 Thomas Burke, in his book *The English Inn*, wrote about this stage of the case as if events happened that defied the nature of human biology, and it is in his text that the business of the hedge-stake being kept at the Sun Inn takes its popular form. The stake became the focus of local ghost stories after that. In a book written just four years earlier, in 1926, *Highways and Byways in Lincolnshire* by Frederick Griggs, there is no mention of Tom Otter in the pages concerning Saxilby.

The inquest came to the conclusion that Mary's killer was easy to locate: the verdict was 'wilful murder against her husband Thomas Temporel'. Poor pregnant Mary was taken for burial at St Botolph's Church in Saxilby, where

The Sun Inn, Saxilby, where the inquest on Mary Kirkham's death was held. (Lincolnshire Library)

5

the vicar, Thomas Rees, said the last words over the grave at the north-east corner of the churchyard.

Of all the early, pre-Victorian murder cases in Lincolnshire, this is the one with the most explicable mythology; instances of servant girls killing their mistresses or poachers shooting gamekeepers are quite common, but there is nothing to rival this case where a man brazenly defied the law and took a life to sort out a legal problem that was weighing heavily on him.

There was a trial and Otter/Temporal was sentenced to hang; this was carried out on 14 March. Baron Sir Robert Graham presided, a man with a massively impressive reputation, as he had been the judge at the trial of the Norfolk man, John Bellingham, who had murdered the Prime Minister Spencer Perceval. There was no real defence, although there was no definite witness (no Dunkerly in sight) and the evidence, gathered from an array of locals, was circumstantial. Nevertheless the jury took only a few minutes to find Tom guilty.

At that time the Cobb Hall tower of Lincoln Castle was the place of execution; it is still there today, dominating the corner of the cathedral car park. The case seems to have been considered so repulsive that something more than a mere execution was required; Otter would have to become a part of the legal mechanism of threat and horror – a standard method at the time, when homicide was so common, of instilling fear into the general populace. Despite the fact that the judge had ordered medical dissection after the culprit's death, he changed his mind and brought in a gibbeting order. This old custom was still very much in use in various parts of the world. In 1783 John Hector St John Crevecoeur described an incident in the Southern states of the USA, writing, 'a Negro who has murdered someone . . . has been suspended in a cage and left to be picked to death by birds of prey, his eyes have been picked out and he is dying from thirst'. This barbaric symbolic warning to malefactors had until recently still been in existence as a permanent fixture much closer to home: in Halifax, the gibbet had fallen into disuse only thirty years before Tom Otter's time. Otter's body was put in a cage that was suspended from a high beam at Saxilby. His remains must have survived there for some time.

It is recorded that the cart with Tom's body in it collapsed as it rattled over the bridge at Saxilby and bystanders were hurt. The crowd following the cart to the gibbet was so excited and frantic that some people were injured in the crush – the Otter myth was being fed. Everything connected to the gibbet would become the stuff of folklore. The Saxilby gibbet stayed there until around 1850 when there was a massive storm. Parts of this terrible object may still be seen by visitors to Doddington Hall, mangled lumps of metal indicative of the awful sight passers-by must have seen in the quiet lane. Fifty years ago Judge Basil Neild wrote about the case in his memoirs, which are always associated with the Otter murder:

Ten tongues in one head.
Nine living and one dead.
One flew forth to fetch some bread
To feed the living in the dead.

The anonymous local poet had also played his part in generating the legend of Tom Otter, a vicious man who chose the wrong time to do that horrendous thing to Mary, to take her life away; he had no idea that the local 'good scout' was just a few yards away, perhaps expecting a voyeuristic thrill but instead suffering a deeply traumatic experience.

In this way began the legend of this case. So powerful and widespread has this been over two centuries that it is not an easy task for the historian to divide the historical facts from the myth. John Dunkerly's statement later on only muddied the waters even further, as his statement begins with reliable data but wanders into the realms of ghost fiction. We are not even sure that Dunkerly was really his name, for some accounts call him Dunberley. The distortions of time and the chronicles of heritage-fuelled tales have veneered the actual historical records with a layer of falsification and old wives' tales. Fortunately for historians of crime, there is enough firm narrative evidence to be sure of the motivations involved, and also of the outcome of the legal process.

2

MP MURDERED BY UNKNOWN HANDS

Lincoln, 1822

This is a tale that many may find more interesting in its speculation than in any certain historical documentation, but it provides a perfect example of that variety of 'suspicious death' for which tantalising evidence of murder exists.

A decade before the Great Reform Act of 1832 began the long process of electoral reform towards the secret ballot (not in existence until 1872) England was beset by problems of local power and corruption. The 'pocket' and 'rotten' boroughs, in which a handful of electors returned MPs to Parliament, were becoming a national scandal. The whole business was one in which factions were created and all kinds of underhand methods were used to secure support from the men of property who had a vote and therefore could be wooed and won by the aspiring politicians. In most cases landed, wealthy local families ran the show. But there was always opposition, which was sometimes from outside, when a stranger would arrive with cash in his pockets to compete with the local power base. A glance at the collection of election posters and leaflets in Lincoln Central Library is enough to confirm the opinion that hustings acrimony and satire were often more vicious than harmless.

In 1800 a chronicle of local events noted that on 9 April, Colonel Sibthorp, MP for Lincoln, invited the inhabitants of the city to dine with him at Canwick. The short description is a masterly piece of 'spin' for a man who had some reason for needing to be seen doing beneficent things in his own 'patch'. But something went slightly wrong, and this was a hint of things to come. The writer goes on to outline the evening: 'A more sumptuous entertainment was never prepared, ample provision for two thousand persons; the gala was so happily preconcerted that every guest would have been entertained but for the licentious conduct of an illiterate rabble which, to the subversion of all comfort, abused the hospitality.'

The Sibthorps were one of the most notable Lincoln families. This particular member was Coningsby Sibthorp, one of the two MPs for the city,

8

the other being Robert Smith, who was the brother of the wit and writer, Sydney Smith. Twenty years after this unfortunate event at his home he was to be embroiled in the repercussions of the national dissensions over the situation of Caroline of Brunswick, former wife of the new king, George IV. After the death of George III in January 1820 the rakish Prince Regent was at last to be crowned the new king. But he was certainly not popular in all quarters, and his attitude to and actions against his one-time queen gained her much sympathy.

It was a time of large-scale fear and even paranoia in the ranks of the government; the coronation took place only a year or so after the terrible massacre of Peterloo in Manchester, where a radical reform gathering to hear

The White Hart Hotel, Lincoln, where Sibthorp stopped for a drink. (Author's Collection)

9

Orator Hunt went badly wrong and the hussars charged the crowd. Into a crowd of over 60,000 went the yeomanry, swords drawn. Eleven people were killed and hundreds were maimed. Amazingly, the local magistrates thought that the soldiers had done very well. Throughout the French Revolutionary years and the Napoleonic Wars there had been increasing fears of sedition and also of gatherings of people. The Combination Acts of 1799 and 1800 had banned meetings in streets of even small knots of citizens. It was risky to stand and chat with a few friends. A group of supporters of a local man would also find themselves in trouble if they spent too long in public and were noisy in expressing their support.

In Lincoln, well before the tragic events of this narrative, there had been trouble at the 1818 elections. *The Times* reported then that 'Lincoln is full of election bustle, three gentlemen having announced themselves as candidates.' One of these was a Londoner, Ralph Bernal, who was a barrister in the Court of Chancery. Sibthorp stood, and he must have seen Bernal as a considerable enemy. The report describes him as a man 'with a gentlemanly demeanour, truly constitutional opinions, well expressed and in animated speech'. Even more worrying for Sibthorp, 'He has certainly gained on the feelings of the citizens.' But it was only the lower orders who paid attention to him (as he distributed his largesse). Sibthorp makes his appearance as 'our worthy member, Colonel Sibthorp, who was present at a party held by his brother to woo the voters'. But again there was mob violence. There were also reports of such tricks as 'wobbling', in which supporters of one man made an intolerable row outside the rooms where canvassing was going on for the other. There were even cases where a barricade was erected outside the White Hart Hotel to try to prevent such occurrences.

There were riots over food shortages and riots over gambling; trouble flared at high prices and at repression of the freedom of speech. But a well-established focus for crowd trouble was the election period and the local hustings. When there was a cause to fight the radicals would take advantage of any situation. Coningsby Sibthorp would be caught up in such a delicate and potentially explosive moment in Lincoln.

The cause of the trouble was the movement for a petition in support of Queen Caroline. The new king had removed Caroline's name from the liturgy, and the coronation in 1821 sparked violence in the streets. Such was the feeling in Lincoln about Caroline's perceived humiliation that the people of the city presented a petition to Parliament in defence of her. Over a thousand names were on it. The public disturbances which were to follow have been described as of enormous symbolic importance. Some would argue that 1821 was a watershed, in that government members actually recognised a public grievance as being worth some attention.

The history of the royal couple had been far from romantic. George married her in order to gain some cash to pay off his mountainous debts,

A SPECIMEN OF

COLONEL SIBTHORP

AS A LAW MAKER!!

The Friends of Humanity are respectfully requested to notice the following Extract from the Essex Independent Newspaper.

We have at different times alluded to the unjust severity of our criminal code; we resume the subject on the present occasion merely for the purpose of exposing a certain gallant member of the House of Commons, who, (did he entertain no other sentiments unpalatable to the people of England but the one to which we are about to allude,) we think, may safely conclude that a Reform in Parliament, whatever it may do for the country generally, will have the effect of speedily expunging his name from the list of British Senators.

A few evenings since, when a Bill was before the House on the subject of the Punishment by Death, Colonel Sibthorp opposed it, and in the course of his observations said,

" He hoped that, next year, the expence of transporting convicts to New South Wales would be lessened at least one third, by the prisoners **BEING CONSIGNED TO THE GALLOWS,** *instead of transporting them to foreign countries !"*

Thus, while the enlightened portion of the community, from one end of the kingdom to the other, are raising their voices in behalf of such measures as shall remove the public burdens from the lower orders of society, and consequently diminish crime, by taking away one of its prolific sources---viz.

EXCESSIVE POVERTY;

Whilst every humane man in the empire is lamenting that the criminal code of England is the most severe in the civilized world; those of the " *Old School*' are straining every nerve to delay the progress of civilisation and good government; and, not content with opposing every measure having for its object the good of the people at large, are seeking to imbrue their hands in the blood of those wretches who are, in many cases, the victims of their own *CORRUPT* Legislation !!

We trust that at the general election, which must succeed the passing of the Reform Bill, all candidates whose sentiments in any degree in unison with those of Colonel Sibthorp will meet with that rebuke to which they are so justly entitled, and be driven from the hustings as men

Unfit to represent the feelings and wishes of a Christian People.

Lincoln, June 16th 1832.

R. B. Drury, Printer, Lincoln.

A handbill against Sibthorp that shows the local opposition to his family. (Author's Collection) then, finding her very unpleasant, refused to live with her. He declared he could not possibly come near her again, so any sexual relations were out of the question. Worse was to follow: word went around that a boy in her company was in fact an illegitimate son whose father may even have been a footman at court. After George III's death in 1820 the government wanted her to stay out of England, but she returned. All the efforts of Henry Brougham, the jurist and politician, to keep her abroad had failed. He had wanted her to renounce the right to be crowned should the king die, and her title of Princess of Wales was to go as well. In 1814 she had taken a sum of money in accordance with some of these terms.

As one anonymous memoirist reported in *Goulding's Almanac* for 1860 there was widespread unrest in the county:

> On Nov 11th, 1820, news that the Bill of Pains and Penalties against the unfortunate wife of George IV had been abandoned was everywhere received with exultation; the people were mostly partisans of the queen; and those of the Lincolnshire towns were very jubilant. There were, however, minorities in all of them, who refused to join in the general illumination of windows. The result was wholesale smashing of panes and other violence by the majorities; indeed, at Grantham the Riot Act was read, and in due course the county was put to considerable expense from broken glass and other damage . . .

At this time Lord Liverpool's ministry was doing very little for Britain. Political reform was looking increasing unlikely under a repressive regime, with spies at work among the working men's clubs and writers of a radical disposition. In this climate, Caroline may well have looked like a cause to fight for, a symbolic representation of gross inequality and unjustness in the establishment of the land. The Lincoln petition was an important part of this. Brougham knew it. He wrote to another politician in August 1820 that Caroline's return would be 'pregnant with every sort of mischief'. How right he was. In Lincoln it led to a murder.

The Lincoln petition was made in February 1821. As Sibthorp would not be involved, it was presented by a man who had been a representative for Lincoln but had now found a constituency in Rochester: Ralph Bernal. But the crucial event in this context was the election after the old king's death that year. Of course, Sibthorp was voted into office, in the usual way of buying votes and with an electorate composed of men largely like him and of his opinions. When he was openly royalist and spoke in Westminster against suffrage reform, he was advertising the reasons for his being so reviled in his own city. Only ten days after the petition fiasco Sibthorp went for dinner to a friend, Dr Cookson, in Eastgate, with his brother and two women family members. Their home was in Canwick and at midnight they were collected to be taken home in a carriage; a journey that led to Sibthorp's painful death.

Someone took the linchpin of the carriage while it was waiting for the dinner guests. On moving off, the vehicle cracked and broke into pieces, which caused the horses to panic, as *The Times* reported: 'On turning into the Minster Yard from Eastgate, the far fore wheel of the carriage flew off and the coachman was in consequence thrown from the box. The horses being frightened immediately became ungovernable and before the coachman could secure them they galloped forward to Miss Ellison's in Minster Yard . . .'

The yard is an area very close to the cathedral, and is largely unchanged today from how it was at that time. It is a small, enclosed space with no roomy exit for a carriage and horses. It is simply an arc, like a small crescent, only 30 feet from the walls of Lincoln Cathedral. The horses must have been very frightened, and the result was that the carriage turned over close to No. 13, crashing through some railings.

Humphrey Sibthorp, the politician's brother, wrote an account of what happened to Coningsby: 'My poor brother was not able to move . . . the injury which my brother received was on the spine and the whole of his left side was paralysed. He was bled and with great difficulty got up to Miss E's [Ellison's] bedroom.' The injuries inflicted condemned the poor man to a long and

Minster Yard, Lincoln, where the carriage overturned. (Author's Collection)

painful dying. The accident took place on 23 February 1821 and Sibthorp died on 9 March 1822. This raises the fine legal point that, were it to be proved that an individual removed the linchpin with an intent to kill, the victim died after the year and a day period allowed by the law for a murder charge to be brought. This is purely academic, of course, but there have been cases where this was a crucially important factor, as with the murder in the twentieth century of Anne Todd of Cottingham who died over a year and a day after an attack on her at her home.

The obituary notice stresses the agonising death: 'Died on Saturday at his home in Canwick, aged 40 years Coningsby Waldo Sibthorp Esq. . . . A long and painful illness he bore without uttering a complaint . . .'

Naturally, a great deal of thought was given to the removal of the pin. The detail that points without doubt to a person intentionally taking out the pin is that the coachman swore he had checked the carriage at Canwick before he travelled to the city, and even more than this, he added some extra ties to the pins. It is a short journey from Canwick to the cathedral Bailgate quarter of the city. It is highly unlikely that the pins could have fallen out in such a journey; had they done so, the coachman would have known immediately. Therefore the carriage had been tampered with while it was waiting. The trouble was that no one could name any specific suspects, though fingers could be pointed at certain quarters of the city's political factions.

It would not have been difficult to remove the pin, and it is most likely that more than one person was involved; two men could take the pin out very easily, and also quietly. It would only have been necessary to distract the driver for a few minutes with some desultory conversation while the nefarious task was accomplished.

Even more indicative of a nefarious act being behind this death is a report of three men heard talking about the crime, saying, 'Here comes the damned carriage' and, 'Let's wait till he's in it and then do it effectively . . .' This tallies well with a note in the account of the coachman's movements that night: he went to fetch Sibthorp from the nearby White Hart Hotel. Sibthorp's travelling such a short distance by coach suggests that he was afraid to walk the streets alone at that time. The other guests were waiting at Dr Cookson's house in Eastgate.

The Sibthorp name continued to be associated with upholding reactionary and unpopular views on many social and political questions. Coningsby's brother Charles stepped into the parliamentary duties, made enemies, caused a stir and was generally noticed for the wrong reasons. The illustration on p. 11 condemns one of his more extreme views, that concerning the benefits of hanging people rather than sending them to penal colonies. The last line expresses the contempt of the Lincoln people, and the feeling must have been the same for his murdered brother: 'Unfit to represent the feelings and wishes of a Christian People.'

It may not be too speculative also to note that in the campaigns for the election in 1823, as bills and declarations were posted all across the city, statements of an extreme tenor were often written, sometimes with strong implications of malpractice and skulduggery, such as one addressed to all freeholders in December, in which the anonymous writer talks of opposing candidates in extreme terms.

As a coda to the story, it should be noted that Caroline of Brunswick died in August 1821, very soon after her return, the cause being what her

GENTLEMEN
Freeholders
OF
THE COUNTY
OF
Lincoln!

I regret much that any advertisements should be issued to find a head for that vain silly body, which, to our own knowledge, has long been contemptible to us, and most mischievous to himself. *No head* can ever supply his body with wholesome food; *no brains* will ever be useful to him. He is a Busy Body—a perfect Marplot. He has long enjoyed the friendship of certain Lords in Yorkshire, Northamptonshire, and Lincolnshire; and never before complained of their unconstitutional kindness to him. They little knew his origin, or would not have confided in him : he was the spoilt and only son of a Quill-driver at Newark. This *body of a Heron*, without any plumage on his back, but with white feathers in his tail, and *the Witham Goose*, his *comrade*, have in a few days hatched a Syston Egg, and from it has burst, in a marvellous manner, a perfect Zany, without any feathers on his back, but a most perfect cap on his head, ornamented with musical Bells. I lament to see this woeful change arise in old Syston Park, where, fifty years ago, no mule bird was to be seen. What will become of this curiosity, time will prove—no honest Freeholder will care; most probably he will be exhibited for a season at Exeter 'Change with Witham Goose and Stubton Heron, and afterwards will be sent to the archives in Coventry, and deposited with Lady Godiva and Peeping Tom.

AN OLD FREEHOLDER.

December 3rd, 1823.

[JACKSONS, PRINTERS, LOUTH.]

A handbill for the election campaign. Elections were often occasions for antagonism and personal feuds. (Author's Collection)

doctor described as 'an indissoluble magnesia of the stomach'. But even at her funeral there was trouble in the streets. The crowd was so rowdy and violent that the cortège had constantly to change its route. There were shouts of 'Bloody murdering rascals' at the law officers. The Life Guards, who had been particularly forceful in their suppression of the rabble, were hailed as 'butchers'.

Lincoln had had its fair share of those rascals just six months previously, and we will never know who they were. In the 1820s all major northern towns had large military garrisons in place. Hull had four companies of fusiliers in 1829; Lincoln itself had the yeomanry. Sibthorp's killing was perhaps just one more in a time when political murders were always likely. He left this world 'by unknown hands' and there was no need for the Riot Act to be read or for troops to stand by for action, although 300 special constables were on hand. The judge for the Midland Circuit arrived the day after Sibthorp's death and nominated John Williams for the seat, an associate of the judge.

The Sibthorp dynasty went on. They were still the main local influence on the political scene; Charles de Laet Waldo Sibthorp held one of the two Lincoln seats from 1826 until his death in 1835. Later, there was open criticism of the family, by W.J. Munson: 'I think it is quite disgraceful the way Sibthorp is always received and the horrid stuff he talks that they cheer.' It may well be that this negative image went back to 1820 when Sibthorp had called a meeting to counter the pro-Caroline faction.

A long dynasty of Sibthorps held power in Lincoln and there was always opposition, but only one attempt at murder, as far as we know. A walker along the lower High Street in the city today, a few hundred yards beyond the railway crossing, will still see the name Sibthorp above some retail premises.

3

A FRIEND MURDERED FOR MONEY

Kirton, 1847

This story begins with a myth rather than with the historical facts, as far as we know them. This myth was featured in the *Scunthorpe Evening Telegraph* in 1954, in a feature headed, 'Legend of Gate where no Grass would Grow.' The piece describes a local legend concerning the villages of Kirton-in-Lindsey and Grayingham, that the grass in the corner of Leonard's Field would never grow. Today this is a very peaceful place, at the junction of a B road and Grayingham Lane, which is little more than a farm track.

The feature reports: 'It is a fascinating yarn that Kirton folk still tell to their children and grandchildren. For the story springs from the town's most notorious murder.' There are many features in the actual narrative about the events of the crime that help us to understand why there should be a myth connected with it. What was essentially a case of two drunken friends falling out led to much more, and the events tell us a great deal about the nature of murder investigations at the time.

A few days before Christmas 1847 Joseph Travis and his friend Charles Copeman went for a drink or two, and they were seen arguing. On the morning after, a Sunday, Copeman was found dead in a ditch in the field, with his head severely bruised, his throat cut and, as the first report stated, 'quite dead'. His dog was found with him, stabbed and bruised. The *Lincoln, Rutland and Stamford Mercury* delivered a detailed account of the discovery of the body on Christmas Eve: 'On Sunday morning at about nine o'clock, as John Whelpton, a labouring man, was proceeding to Kirton along the bridle path leading from Grayingham, his attention was attracted by a dog sitting on something by the road-side which . . . he discovered to be a human body with the face downwards and the dog sitting upon the back. . . . Two other men came up directly but none of them dare approach.'

The man who found the body, a Mr Whelpton, carried out some elementary observations while another man called a constable, and he noted that there were footmarks from the Kirton direction that matched the dead man's boots, and another set of footprints from the east side, joining the victim's. Not far from the body there were obvious signs of a desperate struggle, and also a wallet with two half crowns, a shilling and a sixpence in it.

A crowd had gathered by the time the law arrived. The body was moved, revealing the face of a man all the bystanders would have known. There was a slash on the left of his face that continued down and across the jugular. There was a cut below one eye and another down the side of the face. The nasal bone was broken. The attack had been savage and brutal: his ear was severed and a gash ran from the ear to the throat. As there was no blood on the man's breast, the conclusion was that the wounds had been inflicted when the victim was down on his back.

It was assumed that there had been more than one assailant, and several men were arrested and questioned in Gainsborough, about 10 miles away, on Monday. A handbill was circulated with a reward of £100 for the apprehension of the killer. The local suspects were arrested simply on hearsay concerning their presence nearby that night, or because of their known characters. Joseph Travis, however, emerged as the main suspect, albeit on circumstantial evidence. Travis was twenty-four, a joiner and cabinet-maker, the son of a local farmer. The *Lincolnshire Chronicle* reported on 31 December that Travis was 'respectably connected' but that he had 'for some time led a most dissipated life and has lost considerable sums at card playing'. When questioned, Travis, according to one contemporary reporter, 'gave a statement replete with gross contradictions'.

Copeman had gone to drink at the Red Lion in Kirton, according to the main source at the time, and Travis had been seen quarrelling with him. There was a scrap of blue cloth in the hand of the dead man, and Travis was reported to have worn a shirt of the same colour. In fact, all the clothes seen on the young man that night appeared to have disappeared. Police searched his home, looking for some boots, some 'embossed drab trousers' and the blue striped shirt. There was no trace of any of these. There was a wide and determined search for the blue shirt around the area in the next few days, to no effect. In addition, people confirmed that Travis had been penniless on the Saturday night, and yet had changed a sovereign while drinking the next day.

There were obvious scratches on Travis's face, and when he was closely inspected, it was found that there was a bruise on his right collar bone. There was also a scratch on his throat and on his hand. Travis tried to explain that these had been done when he was taking down a sheep-net a few days before the evening's heavy drinking, but a young boy swore that Travis had not been doing any hedging work. Everything seemed to point to him being the killer.

A girl servant at the Travis home was questioned, and a long conversation at the inquest concerned the nature and whereabouts of three pairs of boots and three shirts owned by the suspect. One of his three pairs had disappeared completely; the servant gave an account of cleaning the other two pairs; and the missing striped shirt was stated to have been worn by Travis on that fatal night. Everything pointed to him as the guilty man, and the discovery of a piece of a penknife blade at the murder scene was the final determining detail. It matched a knife Travis had bought in Kirton on 10 November. He also had three sovereigns on him, and later a fourth was found in the area around the Red Lion where he had been seen searching the ground on the Monday.

Travis was arrested and charged with wilful murder, and this news first emerged at the inquest in Kirton, so it only needed a coroner's warrant to have him taken to Lincoln Castle. C.H. Holgate, one of the county coroners, had presided. There had been an initial enquiry on the Monday, at which several witnesses had been questioned at length, then the inquest was adjourned until the Wednesday. The story was that Travis and Copeman had been drinking at the Greyhound Inn in Kirton with some other men; there had been an altercation in which Travis and Copeman very nearly came to blows. Most of the men moved on to continue the binge at the Red Lion, while Travis stayed on alone at the Greyhound. It is easy to imagine the situation: Travis was very drunk and without cash, whereas Copeman had plenty on him. He had been humiliated and then abandoned by his drinking friends. It was a cold December yet the navvies who had been drinking in the area came out to fight in the streets. While this was going on, Travis was seen

The murder scene, the lane, Grayingham. According to local legend, nothing will grow on this corner of the field. (Author's Collection)

loitering, and he was also seen by Fox's Passage, which leads to the Lincoln road. Later he was also seen talking to Copeman. Copeman then left, walking towards Grayingham.

The reports indicate a considerable problem with what we now call anti-social behaviour. Kirton had grown markedly in this period; the county directory for 1856 notes: 'It increased its population from 1542 in 1831 to 1848 souls in 1851'. Although it could possibly be described most accurately as a large village, it nevertheless had quarter sessions for the North Division of Lindsey, covering a large geographical area, and also its own House of Correction ('Bridewell'). The fighting in the streets that night in late December was not unusual; brutality was often in public display in the place. A few decades before these events a certain William Paddison had 'mayhemmed his wife', meaning that he set out to break both her legs, and did so in front of his own home. After the first leg was broken neighbours intervened to prevent him from breaking the other. Such was the open, unfeeling violence of the times.

The Red Lion, at that time, could be described as one of the main drinking-houses in the village, though it was not on the busy road leading from Brigg to Lincoln; in 1847 it was run by James Shadford, and his enterprise was that of a small-scale coaching house. He rented out horses and gigs. His inn would have been the most spacious of the seven pubs in the village and the most appealing to the local casual labour. The fact that there were navvies drinking there suggests several interesting aspects of the local scene at the time. Labour was always needed for ditching and irrigation work, and also for casual farm work. There are thirty farmers listed in an 1856 directory, including the places where Copeman and Travis worked. Five of these were large, ambitious businesses that were owned by the inhabitants at that time. Casual work in the Brigg–Kirton area was always available. Social problems inevitably followed.

There was always plenty of minor crime going on in Kirton, as the calendars of prisoners show: in 1851, for instance, there were cases of stealing and receiving of heifers; clothes were stolen from private property on several occasions; and there was a considerable vagrancy problem, with men being recorded as 'rogues and vagabonds' around the parish.

In the period 1793–1801, when enclosure took place in the parish, the land awarded to one Robert Travis includes 2 acres, 1 rood and 7 perches. The family was in a small way of business then, but soon grew into a respectable, prominent outfit in the area.

Copeman was buried at Blyborough, a small village just a few miles from Kirton on the Lincoln road. There was a large attendance and there was testimony at the service to Copeman's good reputation in the community. The Revd Graham conducted the service and six of Copeman's servants carried the coffin. As was the local custom, his coffin was taken to the cemetery in a farm wagon.

LINCOLNSHIRE, **LINDSEY TO WIT.**

CALENDAR OF PRISONERS

AT KIRTON OCTOBER SESSIONS,
ON FRIDAY THE 17TH DAY OF OCTOBER, 1851.

The letter *N.* denotes the prisoner cannot read or write.—*Imp.* read, or read or write imperfectly.—*Well,* read or write well.—*Sup.* superior education.
—The letter *h. l.* hard labour.—The asterisk(°) the number of times the prisoner has been committed.—
The parallel lines(‖) those who have been convicted of felony.

READ AND WRITE.	NAMES.	AGE	WHEN COMMITTED	OFFENCES.	COMMITTING MAGISTRATES.	SENTENCES.
Imp ...	1 James Riley	16	July 7th	Stealing at Gainsborough, one Silver Watch, the property of James Whiley.	Rev. G. Hutton	1 C. M. H L
N	2 William Andrews	25	July 12th	Stealing at Gainsborough, three pieces of Silver coin called Shillings, two pieces of Copper coins called Pennys, one other piece of Copper coin called a Halfpenny, and one Gown, the property of Elizabeth Wilson.	Rev. C. W. Hudson	3 C. M. H L
N	3 Mary Ann Andrews	22				
Imp ...	4 John Drury°	23	July 17th	Stealing at Barrow, one Bacon Ham, a quantity of thrashed Wheat, and a Calico Bag, the property of John Robinson.	S. Wormald, Esq.	4 C. M. H. L. Recommended
N	5 James Maw‖°°	24	July 22nd	Stealing at Barton, two pieces of Gold coin called Sovereigns, and seven pieces of Silver coin called Shillings, the property of James Maw, senior.	G. C. Uppleby, Esq.	Acquitted
Imp ...	6 Elizabeth Thompson	60	July 24th	Uttering at Gainsborough, a certain piece of false & counterfeit coin resembling a Crown piece, and having other pieces of false and counterfeit Coin in her posession, well-knowing them to be false and counterfeit.	H. E. Smith, Esq.	3 C. M. H L
Imp ...	7 John Thomas	25	Aug. 1st	Stealing at Haxey, one Brass Pan, the property of Joseph Marris.	Ven. Archdcn. Stonehouse	2 C. M. H. L.
Imp ...	8 Martha Proven, otherwise Martha Eden	37	Aug. 4th	Stealing at Thonock, twelve yards of Carpet, the property of Henry Bacon Hickman, Esq	H. E. Smith, Esq.	4 C M H L
Imp ...	9 William Newton	20	Aug. 16th	Stealing at Hibaldstow, one Waistcoat, one Shirt, and other articles, the property of Thomas Hancen.	Sir J. Nelthorpe, Bart.	4 C. M. H. L. Whipping
Imp ...	10 Valentine Geddins	25	Sept. 1st	Stealing at Willingham, two Heifers, the property of John Hopkinson.	W. Hutton, Esq.	12 C. M. H. L.
Imp ...	11 William Hill	29	Sept. 1st	Receiving at Willingham, the above Heifers, well-knowing them to have been Stolen, the property of John Hopkinson.	W. Hutton, Esq.	12 C. M. H. L.
Imp ...	12 Thomas Hill. acq?	66				Acquitted
N	13 Andrew Hart	48	Sept. 9th	Stealing at Thornton, one Jacket, the property of Charles Kirman.	W. D. Field, Esq.	3 C. M. H L
Imp ...	14 Elizabeth Cummins	27	Sept. 19th	Stealing at Gainsborough, two pair of Stays, five Blankets, one Woollen Scarf, and other articles, the property of John Moore.	Rev. J. T. Huntley, Rev. J. Stockdale	4 C. M. H. L.
Imp ...	15 John Clay		Sept. 25th	Stealing at Snarford, one Cotton Shirt, the property of Matthew Sharman.	Rev. J. T. Huntley	3 C. M. H L
Imp ...	16 James Smith	28	Oct. 9th	Stealing at South Ferriby, one Silk Handkerchief, the property of George Drury.	G. C. Uppleby, Esq.	4 C. M. H.
N	17 John Uffindale	29	Oct. 13th	Stealing at Ealand, two tame Rabbits, the property of George Crowcroft; also stealing at Crowle, one Turkey, the property of John Brunyee; and further charged with stealing at Ealand, one Rabbit, the property of Richard Thornton	G. S. Lister, Esq. Rev. J. Dobson T. H. Lister, Esq.	4 C. M. H. L.
N	18 Henry Stainforth	30	Oct. 13th	Stealing at Ealand, one tame Rabbit, the property of Richard Thornton; also stealing at Ealand, one tame Rabbit, the property of George Crowcroft.	G. S. Lister, Esq. Rev. J. Dobson T. H. Lister, Esq.	4 C. M. H L
Imp ...	19 Macarty Daniel	23	Oct. 14th	At Caistor, did attempt feloniously and burglariously to break and enter the Dwelling-house of William Pybus.	Rev. J. T. Hales Tooke	3 C. M. H. L.
Imp ...						6 C. M. H. L.

A calendar of prisoners, which gave basic information on local criminals. (Lincolnshire Archives)

In Lincoln Castle, Travis wrote to his mother and to a young woman (reputedly his fiancée) in a very defensive way, basically asking them to say very little. He perhaps realised that the evidence was circumstantial and that he had a slim chance of escaping the noose if he was cautious. The trial opened on 4 March 1848. The reports agree that 'the Kirton murder excited great interest', but one reporter complained that 'more bailiffs, more candles and more crown calendars [for the use of the newspapermen] were needed'. It was a *nisi prius* court: the journalist at the time did not know his law, as he called it a '*nici pricus*' and was in a rush to get the dramatic events on paper. This meant a makeshift arrangement whereby the assize commissioners had jurisdiction to hear the full case but had only a delegated power to proceed on certain issues and could not give a judgment. The phrase means 'unless before then', that is, before the King's justices could come to the assize at the regular time. All this suggests that there

Red Lion Passage, Kirton, led to the inn where Travis drank. (Author's Collection)

Little has changed in Blyborough today; it is still a small, quiet village. (Author's Collection)

was haste involved; they had their man and wanted to bring things to a conclusion.

All this implies that the unseemly haste involved meant there was some 'playing the system' by the magistrates. It is unlikely that this stemmed from any public clamour for the normal process of law to be interfered with: rather it was that the magistrates were convinced this was an open and shut case and wanted it out of the way, as by 8 March the court proper would sit. At that trial Mr Justice Maule presided, and indeed there was not enough convincing evidence to convict. Travis, who, according to one reporter, was 'in good health and was well dressed but had a rather repellent exterior', was noted to have been without any clear emotional response, except for one point at which the penknife was discussed. It took the jury an hour and a half to decide that there was insufficient evidence, and Travis walked out into the grounds of Lincoln Castle a free man. This is hard to believe, when we consider that the evidence was circumstantial, and that a common view at that time, held by many principal lawyers, was that such evidence was more or less conclusive. Henry Hawkins, for instance, a celebrated QC of the period, wrote in his memoirs: 'Some writers have spoken of it [circumstantial evidence] as a kind of dangerous innovation in our criminal procedure. It is actually almost the only evidence that is obtainable in all great crimes, and it is the best and most reliable.'

The judge who looked at Travis and directed the jury may also have been a factor. Mr Justice Maule was extremely strict and capable of throwing his weight about. He was remembered by one ex-barrister as 'A man of great wit, sound sense, and a curious humour such as I never heard in any other man. He possessed . . . a particularly keen apprehension.' It seems likely that Maule was not sanguine about circumstantial evidence, and he often allowed general impressions of the community involved with his cases to interfere with his judgments. Quite possibly he had made up his mind about the overall violence and lawlessness in Kirton on this occasion and considered that Travis was simply one of many inhabitants who relished some violence after a heavy drinking session.

Yet this was only the first act of this drama. On 17 March news was announced that Travis was to be arrested again, and that a witness had come forward. This was a bricklayer called Fell, and his words opened up the possibility that Travis could now be arrested for robbery only, if a second trial were to occur. The man said that he had been dozing near the scene of the attack and had heard the fighting. He claimed that he had been given two sovereigns to say nothing about it. Travis had tried to frighten Fell by telling him that accepting a bribe was a serious crime and he would be in trouble. This appears to be a convincing detail, entirely in keeping with what we know of Travis. On 31 March, Travis was in the magistrate's court on a charge of robbery. There was a long list of stolen items: four sovereigns, two shillings, a sixpence, a bunch of keys, a pocket knife and other small items. During a twelve-hour trial at which a long succession of witnesses were called, it was obvious that here was a murderer. The judge closed by pointing out that Travis was guilty of a savage and heartless robbery, and very likely of a murder too. But the trial was for robbery: Travis was sentenced to transportation for life.

However, this was not to be the end of his story. He now had nothing to lose, and made a confession to the murder on 3 August 1848. Varying accounts of his subsequent fate differ greatly. One recent recounting of the case has him dying on board ship for Van Dieman's Land 'a few months later', but another tale has him being shot while trying to swim to freedom. Whatever the truth, his crime continues to resonate in the Kirton area. This appears to begin with the report about Whelpton, who found the body, given on 28 July during the trial: 'A person named Whelpton . . . had some weeks ago a most remarkable dream in which he saw Mr Copeman returning from Kirton late at night, and that between Kirton and Grayingham he was attacked and murdered. He told it to Mr Copeman but he only laughed at his fears. Not long after, Mr Whelpton had the same dream, which affected him so much he went again to Mr Copeman, who promised him he would not return again so late at night, and he did not, until the night of his death.'

Strangely, forty years later, when there were some attacks on the road at Broughton, a few miles away, a key witness was one Edward Whelpton. As for the Copeman and Travis families, they were still there a decade after the murder. By that time Daniel Copeman, the victim's son, was running the farm, and Joseph's parents, George and Elizabeth, were still keeping up their business. Their occasional meetings must have been very strained.

The truth about the legend of no grass growing at the corner of Leonard's Field is that a roadman at the time, whose task was to cut back the roadside vegetation, realised that there was intense public interest in the local murder and kept the crime scene open and flat so that passers-by who wanted to stop and stare could do so with the proper degree of understanding about the site of this brutal killing.

Today the Red Lion is only hinted at by the presence of Lion Passage, a small thoroughfare leading from the central square of Kirton; and the market square as it is now does not easily evoke those wild times when navvies turned out to fight. But much of the village is still as it was then and the geography of this notorious killing can be comprehended by a short walk around the streets and lanes. As the local historian H.A. Fisher has explained, 'Even in Lion Passage leading from South Cliff Road to Market Place, named after the Red Lion pub at its eastern end, had cottages, the steps of which can still be seen in the ground.' In other words, in 1849 people were huddled there in small dwellings. Whatever went on in the street, whether there was a brooding, malevolent man like Travis hanging around on a corner, or a loud and inebriated mob filling the square, would be seen by plenty of local inhabitants.

4

THE LAST PUBLIC EXECUTION IN THE COUNTY

Sibsey, 1859

At its simplest level, this is a story about two young men with plenty of drink in them and desperate for money who set out to rob and kill a man at night in Sibsey. They put on handkerchiefs as masks and set about old William Stevenson, and it led to their being on the scaffold in Lincoln and becoming the men who went down in criminal history as the last people hanged in public in the county.

Along with this goes the disgraceful account of the public behaviour at this time, and also the debate in the first half of the nineteenth century on the whole question of execution. By the 1850s there was an increasing unease among many in Victorian society about the nature of hanging and its processes and traditions. In 1833 an anonymous author, simply described as a schoolmaster who had worked in Newgate, wrote a book with a long discourse on hangings; he had seen many, and on the subject of its being public, he wrote:

> It is then asked may not some tendency for cruel laws originate in a love of excitement, and particularly of that excitement which shares the distress of others. . . . I am quite at a loss to account for the number of respectable persons who consent to be brought to witness the horrible scenes . . . Sometimes the affair takes on quite another turn, and the malefactor is seized with a frenzy for death, as being the only road to happiness. This effect is brought on by the operation of great excitement on weak minds . . .

There was certainly 'great excitement on weak minds' on 5 August 1859 in Lincoln. But the murderous tale begins one night in March 1859 at the Ship Inn in Sibsey. William Stevenson, sixty-four, had been in Boston that day and was enjoying a drink. In the pub at the time were Henry Carey and

26

William Picket, two young men in need of cash. They were talking about their miserable condition, the fact that the world seemed to be unfair to them, and the more they drank the more attractive the possibility of remedying the situation seemed to be, if they were bold enough. The next stage was to choose a victim, and there in the bar was William, a man who had made some money selling pigs. The idea was first expressed by Carey with the words, 'Let's kill the old bastard, I think he's got some money.' They left the Ship before Stevenson, having made a plan to ambush him.

Mary Semper was near the river the next morning and saw what she first thought was a shirt floating in the ditch of a sewer, only a short distance from the old man's cottage. As she approached, however, she saw that it was the bloody body of William. He had terrible injuries to his head.

The narrative of the attack had clear traces: the police found a trail of blood marking where the victim had either been dragged or had been walking as it dripped from him. There were even some blood-marked fence stakes and footprints nearby. There was going to be no problem making an arrest, as people had seen the two men, who had a local reputation as rough characters, the night before. The police found them and there was blood on one boot, with a direct match of their boot prints with those in the mud. Carey even had Stevenson's knife in his pocket. They had beaten the man viciously with the stakes and then thrown him into a ditch. But he was not so easy to kill, and climbed out of the ditch, horrifying them. They had to finish the awful job: after all, they knew him and he knew them. His last words to them were, 'Oh, Picket, what are you doing?'

All this had been done on the expectation of stealing a large amount of money, but the man only had a sovereign on him. Picket, in court, said that had he known that he would have let him pass. The attack had been planned while the two men were full of beer, and game to drink even more, with three pints being put into a jug for them by the landlord before they left. Carey had been the one to conceive of the attack, and he had talked Picket into doing it. The horrendous design on the old man's life grew out of the belief that he had a few pounds on him; that it would be an easy thing to accomplish; and the drink in them filling them with recklessness and bravado.

Carey and Picket were drifters, men with a reliance on either short-lived casual labour or petty crime; their bed for the night on this occasion was to be an old boat, and no doubt they had more beer with them to make sure they had a night's sleep in such discomfort. In court, as questions were asked to obtain more detail about the events of that night, it emerged that Carey had put a lot of thought into the crime. He had said, 'Threepence is all I've got. I must have some money from somewhere.' The two had started quarrelling as they became more drunk, and eventually the landlord told them they had drunk enough and should be going home. When Picket said the old man knew him, Carey was ready with something he had prepared earlier: two handkerchiefs, the one for Picket with holes for his eyes. Carey was not known to Stevenson, so he was not concerned about being seen by him. If there was any doubt about whether or not Carey had indulged in premeditation, it was clarified when these words were spoken at the trial: 'Let's go round by the bridge over the dyke . . .' He knew exactly where the best place would be to wait for the victim. He went on to size up the situation and the likely defence: 'He keeps a good big walking stick; you'll have to hold him while I do the rest.' When Picket said he would not hold the old man, it became obvious that Carey was ready for a fight and knew that he could not lose.

Stevenson was a strong, self-reliant man, well respected in the area. He was at that time living with his son at Sibsey Northlands. This isolated place was described by one reporter at the time as 'so called because the lands are intersected by drains, some large and some small, running in various directions'. It was a long, bare stretch of land and water then. One story told in the 1930s about Sibsey was that the road was so monotonous and uninteresting that a man driving a coach there in the 1860s when the roads were deep and watery asked a local what place it was. He was told 'Stickney' and said, 'We shall all come to Stick neck next!' Stevenson lived at a house just 500 yards from the bridge that the two villains had crossed that night. There was no fence between the road and the sewer on the path to his home.

Stevenson was certainly not drunk when he walked homewards and met Carey and Picket. The killers launched their first attack on him, with the stakes. One stake shattered into pieces, such was the fury of their assault. They then threw him into the ditch, thinking they had battered him to death, but, frighteningly, he came out, coughing and groaning. He had been temporarily revived by the cold water, but it is not clear whether he realised what exactly had happened to him. Picket ran to him and gave the coup de grâce. He was searched and robbed; they found just one sovereign on him and some change; Picket took that, along with the knife, and Carey had the sovereign. They then hid the booty in a hole near the Sun Inn. The drunkards then slept close by, near the house of George Sands. They did not even stagger to the boat they had in mind for a bed.

Stevenson had been very severely battered and was a shocking sight. Mary Semper found the body in the sewer ditch and called in her husband, and then the forces of law. Mr Semper and a man called Coates dragged the body out of the water for closer inspection. The scene of the crime was described in this way by a reporter from the area:

At about 80 yards' distance from the place where the body was found, but on the opposite side of the road, were seen indications of a struggle, trodden grass with blood upon it, and footmarks were observed, apparently made by persons crossing the road, and at the same time dragging with them something heavy. In the ditch that skirted the road were found three broken fragments of a hedge stake marked with drops of blood . . .

There were marks in the sewer mud, and the low hedge that bounded the sewer seemed to have been broken down in one place by someone getting over it. It was also bloody in another part for about a foot's breadth.

When the shattered stake was pieced together, it was over 4 feet long. There were blood and hair on the grass by the side of the sewer, and the old man's son had the misfortune to come across a pool of blood about 12 yards from the hedge, in towards the field. A Sergeant James took control of things and soon found that the two men sleeping by Sands's place were the suspects. It looked as though they had attacked and robbed the old man, and then attempted to drown him in the sewer ditch. The marks of the struggle clearly conveyed the sequence of events and the killers' increasing desperation when the man proved to be an indomitable opponent.

Carey had said to Picket when he planned the walk across the bridge to the place of ambush, 'That's what I wanted you for.' In other words, the 'malice aforethought' was meticulous and the idea expressed clearly even though he was drunk. But at the Crown Court of the Midland Circuit, Fitzjames Stephen for the prosecution made it explicit from the start that both were

Castle Prison, Lincoln, the destination of Biggadike and many others. (Author's Collection)

equally to blame. *The Times* reported: 'After a few introductory remarks, he stated to the jury the facts by which the case on the part of the Crown would be conducted . . . commented with great minuteness upon a statement made by the prisoner Picket . . . tended to show that Picket himself was present upon the spot when the deceased, Stevenson, was by some persons attacked and killed.' It soon became apparent that this prelude to the case was because Picket had been advised, as he was defended by Mr Macaulay and Mr Flowers, to push the blame towards Carey, who was in fact undefended. Picket's long statement in the dock was biased towards showing Carey as the originator of the murderous plan and himself as a weak, docile figure who became more so when he had taken a few pints of ale.

Carey was silent throughout the trial and never asked a single question of anyone. His account of the day reinforces the view of the two men as being rootless and subject to the whims of the employers around them: Picket had told how he worked for Mr Sands for a few days, staying with him, and that he would be locked out if he did not leave the Sun by a certain time. It had been market day and plenty of people were drinking after a long day's work. Was Picket an accomplice, or an accessory after the fact? For a long time on 27 July he spoke at length about how he was advised when first arrested at Stickney to say nothing; that he was a passive individual who had been easily led by a more aggressive and wayward character. If Carey was angry at having to stand in court and hear all this from a 'grass', then he was impressively self-controlled.

Picket's defence lawyers were amazingly active in their efforts to ease their client's condition and how he was perceived in the court. They even said that if common justice regarding the circumstantial evidence incriminated him, then consideration should be given 'to other things that tended to limit the degree of his criminality'. By this they meant that there were suggestions that Stevenson had used Picket harshly in the past, and that his nature had perhaps been made more harsh and unpleasant by him having been given notice to quit from his previous property. All this was very complicated and smacks of being a desperate last-ditch attempt to find some vestige of sympathy for Picket, if at all possible. If there was doubt about Picket there was none about Carey, at least in the mind of the *Lincolnshire Chronicle* writer who said that he had 'a low forehead, thought to distinguish murderers'.

Another factor was the atmosphere in the court at Lincoln. The first day of the trial was particularly hot and humid; the jury, having to listen to all this detail and speculation in order that they might compare the two men and begin to see some differences, was under stress. The judge, Mr Justice Williams, adjourned the trial until the next day, and the jurors were escorted around the corner to the White Hart Hotel for the night, to recover.

The next day matters were soon brought to a close. It took the jury just twenty-five minutes to make a decision. Both men were found guilty. When sentenced, Picket said, 'My father has often told me that if I kept company with Carey I should be transported or hanged.' It is particularly ironic that he also made a point of saying how much he had liked the victim: 'It is all drink . . . Mr Stevenson was always a friend to me. He took me in when I was turned out of my own house.' Carey then confessed that he was really responsible for urging Picket to be involved. But none of this mattered; they were going to be hanged by William Calcraft.

On the day of execution it was noted that they fully confessed their guilt and 'manifested the greatest repentance'. This last public execution in the county was perhaps the worst example of mass hysteria and gruesome fascination with the drama of the scaffold. There were disgraceful scenes at the event, on 5 August 1859. The landlords of two public houses nearby in Bailgate, the Plough Inn and the Yarborough Arms, made their front yards viewing areas, with an admission charge of 3d for those citizens who wanted a good view of the Cobb Hall tower from where the two men would be suspended, which irritated local reformists. Today it is hard to imagine this, as there has been a building development of shops and restaurants by the castle car park, but as the visitor walks from the car park through to Bailgate he walks beneath Cobb Hall, and the projecting spar of stone may still be seen from the centre of the tower. In 1859 there would have been a flat stretch of land between what is now a preserved Roman pavement in the Bail, all the way to the corner of Cobb Hall by the castle fortifications. It would have been a very large open area, enough to hold thousands of spectators.

Around that area in 1859 the crowd packed in to gaze upwards, to listen to any dying speeches, and to take a sick, voyeuristic pleasure in seeing the two murderers hang. Pickpockets worked in the ranks of the people; the *Lincolnshire Chronicle* noted that several notorious thieves were there to make some easy profits. The writer for that newspaper expressed his disgust:

> It is almost impossible to believe that men following a respectable position in society would be guilty of so discreditable an act and that men could be found to patronise them. But so it was, and judging from the numerous persons who paid their three pence, we have no doubt the landlords made a considerable sum of money. Before twelve o'clock every spot where a sight of the gallows could be obtained was filled with a crowd so dense that it was almost impossible to penetrate through it.

This event was the last of a centuries-old traditional English entertainment, and we have a clear picture of the opinion of them in mid-Victorian Britain. Some commentators saw these affairs as an opportunity for repentance and an assertion of faith. When there was no religious content, men of the cloth were not happy, as in Lincoln on this occasion when a local clergyman tried to exhort the noisy crowd to more sober and appropriate behaviour.

He went on record in the newspaper as saying, 'There is generally much drinking, bad language and thoughtlessness, and cruel laughter when the unhappy criminals are punished.' He had an explanation: that sinful men 'cannot bear to look calmly at so awful a sight as the death of a fellow creature so they excite themselves as if they were at a place of amusement'.

A contrasting opinion of the scaffold tradition was to see it as rebellion. In street literature and song, the notion of the unrepentant criminal, the man who puts two fingers up to the law, always had a place. Robert Burns's song, 'Macpherson's Farewell', expresses this in the lines:

> There's some have come to see me die,
> some to hear me play.
> But Macpherson's time will ne'er be lang
> On yonder gallows tree.
> So rantingly, so dauntingly played he . . .

The old public spectacle of the days of Jack Sheppard and the parade to Tyburn, in which defiance, not repentance, was the order of the day clashed with the aspirations and radical ideas of Victorian religion and philanthropy. Thomas Hardy, when he was sixteen (in 1856), watched the public execution of Martha Brown, and as Robert Gittings relates: 'In 1919, with Lady Ilchester and daughter, he recounted the terrible details, told him by an ancestor, of the burning of Mary Channing, the murderess . . .'

However, whatever the opinions were of their spectators, Carey's and Picket's deaths were unremarkable. There were no scenes of high drama, no defiance. Their executioner, William Calcraft, had started out as a lad, by selling pies at public hangings. Later he made a success of his career as a hangman, being paid £1 a week retaining fee by the City of London and over £5 from Surrey. He retired in 1874. Oliver Cyriax explains the contribution made by this man to the rituals of the trade in his *Encyclopaedia of Crime*: 'Calcraft hanged people off a three-foot drop, and indulged in one of the more peculiar ruses to segregate his personal from his professional life. On arrival at a prison for a hanging garbed in a black suit, he would change his clothes, donning another black suit of identical design . . .'

Three years before this last execution in Lincoln a Royal Commission recommended the ending of this degrading spectacle; the panel of professionals saw that any deterrent effect such punishment might have was far outweighed by the dangers and social problems generated by the attendance of large crowds. The last public execution in England took place in Newgate on 26 May 1868. Another radical change in the law occurred just two years after the deaths of Carey and Picket. This was the Offences Against the Person Act of 1861. This legislation meant that finally the death penalty was abolished for all crimes except murder and high treason.

5

POISONED BY PRISCILLA AND MARY?

Mareham-le-Fen and Wrangle, 1868/1884

Arsenic has been the favourite of poisoners for centuries. The oxide occurs in nature in a variety of substances, and as white oxide of arsenic it can be given in almost any form. Arsenic stays in the body for a very long time and, when placed in food, the smell is easily disguised. Also, the symptoms of the victim can be similar to those of dysentery and cholera. For these reasons, and the fact that it was easily available in rat poison and fly-papers, it became a factor in hundreds of recorded poisoning cases in the nineteenth century, and surely many more that were never recorded. Family doctors would all too often record another cause of death.

Arsenic came to be considered so dangerous in the wrong hands that by the middle of the Victorian period steps were taken to try to limit the abuses of it. The Arsenic Act of 1851 was an attempt to control the sales of the poison; too many tradesmen had set up as 'druggists' and were not really controlled by any professional standards. The Act made it necessary first for the buyer of the arsenic to be known to the retailer, and second that the substance must be mixed, commonly with indigo, and pinkish coloured. Soot was also permissible as a colorant.

As far as Lincolnshire is concerned, all this is very relevant; the statistics show that poisoning offences were far more frequent in the east of England in the nineteenth century than in other provinces. Prosecutions and sentencing were severe in the extreme. Katherine Watson, in her book *Poisoned Lives* (2004), notes: 'Before 1838, almost every poisoner under sentence of death was executed. After that year only murderers were ever hanged, and over 40% of poisoners had their death sentences commuted. From 1837 to 1868 inclusive, 347 murderers were executed in England and Wales, around 10% were poisoners.' In Lincolnshire there were four notorious poisoning murders and around eight suspected attempted murder cases involving arsenic that went to the assizes, and most were dismissed.

Two Lincolnshire poisonings have been widely studied. Both prisoners were women from small rural communities. Mary Lefley was most likely innocent and wrongly hanged, and Priscilla Biggadike has since been shown to have definitely been innocent. The following events are therefore tragic and disgusting, but were in accordance with the workings of the law and of investigations in that era.

In 1868 the village of Mareham-le-Fen, about 6 miles south of Horncastle, was a small parish close to Wildmore Fen; the population was about 480; listed as notable residents in the 1850s are 15 general retailers and 17 butchers. In other words, it was simply a place where people scraped whatever living they could, many existing close to the level of what was then called the 'underclass' – a term embracing many categories of person from poacher to general casual labourer.

One family group, though a strange one, was that of Richard and Priscilla Biggadike. Priscilla was born in Gedney and married Richard in 1855. In 1868 they were existing in a ramshackle hut at Stickney; she was twenty-nine and her husband a year older. They had three children and also two lodgers, George Ironmonger and Thomas Proctor. The latter was a rat-catcher (they were often employed by the corporation at a set fee per tail). All lived under the same small roof, using two beds just 18in apart. Ironmonger was in the

Priscilla Biggadike in a sketch by Laura Carter.

habit of taking Mr Biggadike's place in the marital bed when the husband went out to work. Naturally problems arose from this. There were domestic arguments and altercations as time went on.

In 1868 the suspicion was emerging that the last Biggadike child was Proctor's. The picture of the Biggadikes' life is one of hardship and strife; village people speaking about them later said that they often quarrelled. Richard Biggadike was usually out at work all day, and his wife was left in isolation with the chores.

This picture of Priscilla's life is very important: a moment's reflection on it reveals the pressures she was under and how she must have had to behave in such circumstances. For instance, the nature of the liaison with the lodger never really emerged from the investigations, but his sexual attentions were more than likely forced upon her. She would have had to work every waking minute to feed, clothe and support the men in this *ménage à trois*. After all, they were living at the basest level, hand to mouth and in a condition of extreme deprivation.

On 30 September 1868 Richard Biggadike ate a meal of hot cakes and mutton made by Priscilla. Mortally ill, he then took to his bed and died after eleven hours of agonising pain and retching. There was no doubt in the doctor's mind at the inquest that this was a case of arsenic poisoning. Priscilla switched the focus to Proctor at the trial, saying she had seen him put a powder into the food. She also claimed the powder was added to a medicine Biggadike was taking. Her story became more convoluted, and when Proctor was shown to have no motive for doing such a thing, a Grand Jury found him innocent. There were only Priscilla's allegations against him.

She claimed that Richard had stated that he wanted to end his own life because he had large debts, and she said she had found a suicide note written by him. But here was a slip: her husband could not read or write. A reported statement by Priscilla, 'I cannot abide him. I should like to see him brought home dead', was the most conclusive point made by the prosecution. There had been frequent violent quarrels between the couple, and they were made part of the case against her.

The inquest, held on 3 October, heard a statement from Dr Maxwell saying that he was called to the home at seven in the evening of 30 September, and that he 'found [Richard Biggadike] in great pain in bed, sick and violently purged. He had all the symptoms of poisoning by some irritant.' At a post-mortem examination the next morning, Maxwell confirmed death by poison and said he was convinced arsenic had been used in a very large dose. He commented, 'There was enough left in the body to destroy the life of another person. I never saw a clearer case of death by poison.'

Priscilla had been placed in the House of Correction, where she had a miserable time: the place was reported as having 'offensively unhealthy cells ten feet by eight . . . the only admittance of light is through a tiny niche in the wall'. She talked to the Governor, John Farr Phillips, and implicated Proctor. Her words seem precise and detailed, at least on the surface: 'On the last day of September I was standing against the tea table, and saw Thomas Proctor put a white powder of some sort into a tea cup, and then he poured some milk, which stood upon the table, into it. My husband came into the room directly after, and I poured his tea out, and he drank it, and more besides . . .' She then gave more information about Proctor putting something else into Richard's medicine bottle. She then tested it: 'As soon as he left the room I poured some medicine into the cup and gave it to my husband, and tasted it myself. In an hour afterwards I was sick, and I was sick for two days after . . .'

All this is peculiarly confusing, as her actions do not seem entirely reasonable or logical. She went on to say more about Proctor, to such an extent that Superintendent Wright of Spilsby charged Proctor with the murder, at which he stated his innocence. Priscilla added the information about the suicide note, saying she had burned it. When Wright insisted that Richard was illiterate, she said, 'No, someone must have done it for him.' Most of her statements were very difficult to uphold, and the general manner of her delivery of this material only built the case against her more strongly. The tiny detail about the note is the one thing about Priscilla that has persisted to this day. The tours guide in Lincoln Castle informs visitors that Priscilla made this 'fatal mistake' about the illiteracy of her husband. But this is by no means as simple as it seems, for someone may well have written it for him. If this was a suicide he would genuinely want the people left behind to understand, and indeed to suffer some guilt and remorse.

But this is modern thinking, and at the time things were seen as much more straightforward. The jury did not take long to return a guilty verdict of wilful murder against both defendants. They were both committed to attend Lincoln Assizes, and were taken to the House of Correction in the meantime. Priscilla was refused any bail.

At the assize trial Mr Justice Byles presided and, although he noted the circumstantial evidence, he expressed his certainty of the simplicity of the case and the obvious guilt of the prisoner. He asked the jury why they recommended mercy, and they simply said that there were 'circumstantial grounds'. Clearly he took no notice of this opinion. Proctor was acquitted and the case went on relentlessly against Priscilla. Proctor had really only said that he was a rat-catcher and that he kept ferrets: he was a one-dimensional man whose nature was never really examined. All the focus was on Priscilla. The *Lincolnshire Chronicle* reported: 'She showed not the slightest emotion throughout the hearing of the trial, and she only made a small show of grief when the sentence was passed on her.'

George Ironmonger tried to visit her but was refused; some of her own family did see her but could not talk her into admitting guilt. We have a

Lincoln Assize Court is still used as a court today. (Author's Collection)

great deal of information about her time in gaol and her execution. She was attended by a chaplain, the Revd W.H. Richter, who was with her most of the time until the hour appointed for the execution: 9 a.m. on 28 December 1868.

Walking out, she wore a white cap, black gown, stockings and boots. She made a moaning noise as she walked. The hanging was to be out of the public eye, on a scaffold by the County Hall, where the chaplain asked her, 'Do you still persist in your declaration of innocence and have you anything to do with the crime in thought, word or deed?' Priscilla simply replied, 'No, I have not, sir.' She was, in the words of Richter, 'left to God' without repentance.

Lucy Tower, Lincoln Castle, where the bodies of the condemned were taken. (Author's Collection)

The Times (29 December) gave a rather different report to that of the local press: 'On finally parting with the Governor and chaplain she shook hands with them. The governor asked her whether she admitted the justice of her sentence. She murmured something – one of the warders thought it was an affirmative reply, but the precise words could not be heard. A few seconds before she had exclaimed, "Oh! You won't hang me!" Everything being in readiness the executioner proceeded to complete his task.'

When the Minster clock, Big Tom, struck the hour, the bolt was slid out and the trap lowered. Thomas Askern, the hangman from York, had been as inefficient as he usually was. He was in the habit of tying the knot under the chin, not at the side under the ear. Askern executed the infamous Mary Ann Cotton in Durham four years after this visit to Lincoln, and just a few months before this Lincoln job he had hanged a teenager in Dumfries. Priscilla Biggadike therefore took three minutes to die. Her last words were reputedly 'Surely all my troubles are over!'

There had been a Capital Punishment Amendment Act in 1868, and this case followed hard on it, so some of the new rules about execution procedure were meticulously followed, the most dramatic being the ritualistic nature of some of the guidelines: 'The bell of the prison or the bell of the parish church . . . to be tolled for fifteen minutes before and fifteen minutes after the execution' and 'A black flag to be hoisted at the moment of execution'. Lincoln possessed all these trappings of a formal state execution.

The closure of the case is what everyone concerned must have feared: the hanged woman was innocent. In 1882, on his deathbed, Thomas Proctor confessed to the murder. Unfortunately this fact has not permeated popular history. In the 1970s three accounts of the story were in print, and these give great emphasis to the simplicity of the poisoning element and accept motives for the wife to kill the husband. These accounts focus on the common use of poisons at the time and Priscilla's use of them: '. . . another woman who had been offered arsenic – which she called white mercury – to kill mice by Priscilla four months before Biggadike's death. Proctor . . . had visited this woman after the death and warned her, "Mind what you say." To which she had replied, "Do you think I'm a fool that knows naught?"' Clearly this kind of writing, making it seem as though Priscilla was some kind of local expert on killing vermin, can make her seem exceptional. In fact she was no different from any other country wife. Using poison would be common practice, and local chemists would no doubt bend the law with regard to retailing arsenic when they were selling regularly to familiar faces.

But all this has no bearing on the execution. The event is told briefly in this paragraph from *Ward's Historical Guide to Lincoln* (1880): '1868 Dec. 28th. Priscilla Biggadike, for the murder of her husband by poisoning on the 1st October. This wretched murderess was the first that was hung under the Private Executions Act, which was strictly adhered to, the officials of the prison

Wrangle Village. (Lincolnshire Library)

and four reporters being the only persons present, beside the chaplain, sheriff and Askern the executioner. She protested her innocence to the last.' From the tower of the castle the black flag was raised. One coda to the story is that a warder, Mary Fox, had given Priscilla a handkerchief as the sentence was passed on her. Long after the case Fox was visiting Madame Tussaud's and found Priscilla Biggadike's effigy there, with a handkerchief in the hand: it was the one Fox had given her prisoner.

Sixteen years later, in the village of Wrangle, there was a strangely parallel case: it involved Mary Lefley, aged forty-nine, and her husband William, a cottager aged fifty-nine. They were living in a freehold property and seemed reasonably happy, as far as the neighbourhood was aware. On 6 February 1884 various friends called at their cottage and everything seemed normal. Mary set off for Boston to sell produce, and later in the day, at about 3 p.m., William arrived at the home of the local medical man, Dr Bubb. Lefley was extremely ill and the doctor was not there. He staggered in and hit the floor, retching and moaning. He had brought a bowl of rice pudding and told some women present that the food had poison in it.

When he was told again that Dr Bubb was not at home, he said, 'That won't do. I want to see him in one minute, I'm dying fast.' A Dr Faskally (the locum) then came and examined him; it was a desperate situation yet for some reason the doctor had Lefley carried to his own home.

When Mary came home that evening her behaviour was confused and to some irrational, which was to have serious repercussions later on. She actually stated to the doctor that she expected Lefley to claim that he had been poisoned. What was then reported about her is strange indeed. A neighbour, Mrs Longden, was present, trying to offer support, and she offered Mary tea. Mary said, 'I've had nothing all day because I felt so queer.' Then she talked about making the pudding: 'He told me not to make a pudding as there was plenty cooked, but I said I always make a pudding and would do so as usual.' In themselves, these two statements are quite innocuous, but in the context of the later trial they were to prove lethal for her.

Other witnesses talked of Mary's references to her husband's attempts at taking his own life. She must have shocked her neighbours when she said, 'It's his badness. He's been a brute since Christmas . . .' Then she added that

Biggadike's gravestone. Barely visible today, this is where Priscilla lies with other unknown felons. (Author's Collection)

one day recently he had gone out with the intention of hanging himself. When questioned about this, Mary said that she had not followed him into the yard after he had said he intended to take his life. Odd though this was, the focus was really on the poison, and no-one could explain where it had come from. A screwed-up paper was found with white powder in it, but it proved not to be arsenic. The Lefleys' behaviour has all the hallmarks of a couple in depression with profound problems in their relationship and in their personal sense of identity and well-being. Mary even described, in a convoluted way, an experience on the wagon going to Boston that suggests she was under mental strain. She explained that she had forgotten why she was going and had a deep sense of confusion.

At Lincoln Assizes on 7 May 1884 she was in the box; there was no other suspect. The police were convinced there had been foul play and she was the obvious culprit. She had been charged on circumstantial evidence only. She pleaded not guilty, and then had to listen to an astounding piece of medical information from the post mortem. There had been a massive amount of arsenic in the rice pudding: over 135 grains. A fatal dose needs only to be two grains. Despite the fact that the white powder found in her home was shown to be harmless, witnesses were called and the trial proceeded. The strangest testimony came from William's nephew, William Lister, who recounted an argument between the couple on 1 February, when his uncle had been drinking a great deal of ale. Uncle William came to his nephew's bed in the night and told him that he had just attempted suicide.

Other witnesses said they had heard Mary say that she wished her husband was 'dead and out of the way'. It was going to be a tough challenge for the defence and the best they could do was take up the data regarding the man's attempted suicide and strive to show that his death was a successful suicide. But the judge had noted the strange, indifferent behaviour of Mary at the time her husband was dying and thought it very odd that she did not go to the man's bedside when his death was inevitable.

She was sentenced to death, and her reply was, 'I'm not guilty, and I never poisoned anyone in my life.' Patrick Wilson, writing in 1971, makes a strong case for her innocence and lists eleven anomalies in the investigation, all pointing to the utter irrationality of the judgment. The main objections are that the man must have noticed the taste of such a massive amount of arsenic in the pudding; there was no indication that the Lefley marriage was suffering problems; and Mary had no access to any poison.

There is also a great deal of helpful detail in the memoirs of the hangman, James Berry from Bradford, a man with much more intellect, sensitivity and consideration than Thomas Askern, the bungler at Biggadike's hanging. Berry was aware that William Lefley was something of a simpleton; he worked as a carrier, and his approach to business made him enemies and brought him ridicule. There were factors about this that never came up at Mary's trial, and

A melancholy view of the cemetery inside the tower itself. (Author's Collection)

Berry, new to the job and keen to do things right, was of the opinion that he was about to hang an innocent woman. But he was a professional with a task ahead of him and he carried on. He wrote his own account of the process in his memoirs:

> To the very last she protested her innocence, though the night before she was very restless and constantly exclaimed,'Lord, Thou knowest all!' She would have no breakfast and when I approached her she was in a nervous agitated state, praying to God for salvation . . . but as an innocent woman . . . she had to be led to the scaffold by two female warders.

Berry records that Mary was ill when he went to fetch her on the fateful morning. She also shouted 'Murder!' Berry wrote with feeling and some repugnance about the whole business, and at having to pinion her. Her cries were piercing as she was dragged along to the scaffold. As Berry reported, 'Our eyes were downcast, our senses numbed, and down the cheeks of some the tears were rolling.' After all, as soon as Berry arrived at the gaol a woman warder had said to him, 'She has never ceased to protest her innocence. Oh Mr Berry, I am sure as can be that she never committed that dreadful crime. You have only to talk to the woman to know that . . .' Berry noted that he 'found the gaol in a state of panic when [he] arrived'. He recalled that the chaplain's prayers had sounded 'more like a sob' on the fateful morning.

The final irony is the dark and troubling parallel to Biggadike's tale, if we believe James Berry, because he relates that a farmer, who had been humiliated by Lefley in a deal, confessed to the poisoning on his deathbed. He said he had crept into the cottage on that day and put the poison in the pudding.

6

PARISH CONSTABLE MURDERED

Hemingby, Horncastle, 1876

The Lincolnshire police force was formed in January 1857, with a manpower of 207 officers led by Capt Philip Bicknell. Before that time and indeed well after its formation the everyday police work in the remote villages of the county were supervised by parish constables. The small village of Hemingby, near Horncastle, has the dubious distinction of being the place where the last parish constable was murdered. This story of the killing of Constable Thomas Bett Gell is notable for two reasons: it took place in an area that had a unique local history of policing, and it involved a classic narrative of the Victorian criminal justice system when it came to understanding insanity.

The victim was a parish constable, an office with a very long history. In the reign of Edward I a law was made placing two constables in each parish, though this was not eagerly enforced; then in 1285 the Statute of Westminster began the 'watch and ward' approach to crime patrolling: basically a night watchman who was to be alert late at night and in the early hours. But by the mid-Victorian period, rural areas still presented a tough problem for the local forces of law and order.

As research by historian B.J. Davey has shown, Horncastle had a most interesting policing structure in the years between 1838 and 1857. Because of an obscure Act of Parliament, the Lighting and Watching Act of 1833, the town in the Lincolnshire Wolds organised and paid its own constabulary. A young lawyer, Richard Clitherow, kept detailed records of the police functions and of crimes for almost twenty years, and we have a rich understanding of the nature of crime in the town.

Just before policing was revolutionised in 1857 Bicknell took up the post of Chief Constable: he was the one Chief Constable for the county, but the ultimate aim was to have one person in that office for each area. A fundamental problem, and it was one which was to have a bearing on this case, was the fact that Bicknell could not transfer a man to another area without the officer losing his pension rights. This was not remedied until 1865.

Difficulties like these were behind the cumbersome process of having a full-time officer close to the thousands of scattered villages across Lincolnshire, to help the amateurs when needed. Bicknell, who retired in 1902, was the man most responsible for improving the policing administration in the county, but his efforts came too late for the constable in tiny Hemingby.

The constable featured in this story had been selected according to Bicknell's requirements. When he looked for a constable for the force he was anxious to recruit the right kind of man; his criteria were principally that the man should be clean, active, intelligent and of 'good height and well made'. Bicknell actually wrote an instruction book, *Bicknell's Police Manual*, and in that one of his directives was that each member of the force 'with his wife and children, is to attend service every Sunday, unless there be good reason to the contrary, and his children are to be sent to school'.

In Bicknell's long reign the Hemingby murder was one of the worst experiences he had – and that includes riots in Lincoln in 1862 and several high-profile murders. Thomas Bett Gell's death pinpointed the weaknesses of the attempts to police such a massive rural area. B.J. Davey, in the study referred to above, which was concerned with the years shortly before the new county and borough police, makes it clear that the Horncastle force, covering Hemingby and other villages nearby, had a wide and demanding remit and a formidable range of crimes to deal with. The police notebooks Davey used for his study show that there was a very high incidence of violent crime. He

Thomas Bett Gell, a police constable in Hemingby, is buried in the graveyard of St Margaret's church in the village. (Lincolnshire Library)

The Ran Tan at Hemingby, where local wrong-doers were punished. (Lincolnshire Library)

says something very relevant to the Gell case that helps us understand how vulnerable and hard-worked the constable was:

> The people of Horncastle were usually not very worried about serious crimes like robbery and they did not expect the likes of Ackrill and Gapp [previous constables a few decades before Gell] to be able to do much about such things anyway. They wanted the policeman to deal with the lawless and immoral, to reduce drunkenness, vice and considerable disorder throughout the town . . .

Country towns always had their problems of social order and crime was often public and in the streets. While London was developing the status and workings of the first 'Peelers' after Sir Robert Peel's Police Act of 1830, and the Metropolitan Police were born, the provinces continued to cope for several decades with part-timers in the constabulary. Many of the crimes that came along as part of the aftermath of the Industrial Revolution were related to an expanding population and the emergence of a more numerous and diverse group of disenchanted and socially excluded people. In the case of Horncastle it was, as Davey states, a large and unruly generation of 15 to 30-year-olds: 'They may . . . have been less subject to certain social controls than their eighteenth-century predecessors: apprenticeships were decreasing; fewer young people "lived in" with their employers . . . some were unemployed and many were chronically under-employed because there was less work available as the country crafts and trades declined . . .'

The constables in the town spent a great deal of time on minor matters: public health risks, minor assaults, youths loitering in dark corners and so on. There were also gangs of villains who were at times real threats to order and safety. By the end of the period one of the last Horncastle constables, Mr Tooms, was energetic in finding a weekend assistant; there were clearly problems with such things as 'noise in a bawdy house' and the pubs abusing the gaming laws.

The duties of a parish constable were onerous and included the supervision of prisoners, putting them in stocks or securing them in a lock-up, and taking them before the magistrate when the time came. He would not usually even have a uniform, and had only a wooden truncheon to symbolise his office or to instil fear. Nevertheless the constables coped well. In 1876, when policing had been radically changed in many parts of the country, the villages clustered around Horncastle still relied on the local constable; in Hemingby the officer was a blacksmith when he was not on duty, and of course he was always on call in emergencies. In the 1871 census he is listed as a wheelwright master employing two men and two boys. One of his fellow tradesmen was to become his killer.

What Gell was faced with when he was killed was nothing ordinary, and needed experts and a force of men to deal with it. This was not possible: Gell was alone.

On 15 October 1876 the blacksmith William Drant, a man with a long history of violence and savage mood-swings, came home after a night of heavy drinking. His wife had left him some time before, and was living with his mother at the time of this affair. He had brought home a family friend on the night in question. At first all was well but he began to change mood and become loud and abusive. This happened after he had complained of feeling ill, had been taken to the house of a Mrs Goddard for some sort of help and been taken home again. At home he lay down and tried to sleep, but after half an hour he woke dangerously aggressive.

Drant, thirty-seven years old and very sturdy and strong, started to rant about Mrs Goddard trying to poison him; she was extremely patient and tried her best to help him and quieten him, but he got to his feet and threatened her with his fists. From that point on his behaviour can only be called manic. *The Times* reported it in these terms: 'He then called for his mother, who, taking alarm, had run out to find assistance. He went out to fetch her and returned, dragging her by the neck into the kitchen of the house where he flung her on to the floor, kneeling on her, taking out a knife and threatening to murder her . . .'

The situation then escalated into open confrontation as four neighbours arrived, two carrying wooden rails from a fence. They wrestled him away from his mother and took the knife. One managed to crack Drant on the head and this almost stopped him, yet he recovered and hit back, narrowly missing one of his assailants.

The next stage was an attack on another blacksmith of the village who obviously knew him. It is not clear whether this man, Leggit, tried to appease the rabid Drant or to tackle him, but he was threatened and ran off. There was so much noise in the street by this time that Constable Gell was roused and arrived just as Drant ran out into the street, swinging a piece of rail. He struck Gell with considerable force. One witness reported: 'It felled him to the ground and repeated blows were heard, sounding as if striking an empty barrel.' The officer was dying, his brain severely damaged. A doctor attended him, but there was no hope and he died the next morning.

While the victim was battling for life Drant had been caught and carried off to the Horncastle lock-up, the Roundhouse, after being arrested by PC Lawson from nearby Baumber (1½ miles away), one of the 'new police'. He was charged with assault and attempted murder. His only reply was a deranged one: 'They have worked me up so much I couldn't stand it a minute longer, watching and peeping about my house, and I've given Gell one.' What emerged later was that Drant had once been employed by Gell, and had been sacked. There was bad blood between them and witnesses stated that Drant had spoken aggressively against Gell on several occasions. But now, in the lock-up, he began to change mood and eventually said, in a more sober tone, 'Oh dear, oh dear, I am sorry. I did not think I had killed him!' This was said as he was charged with murder at the inquest, held at the Coach and Horses pub at Hemingby, and the charge of wilful murder meant that he was on his way to the next Assizes.

The trial was on 29 December and Baron Huddleston presided. The prosecution was led by Barnard and Lumley, and the man charged with assembling some kind of defence was Horace Smith. Smith tried his best to approach the issue by way of the theory of insanity, referring to the fits to which the accused was subject. Apart from that, his most applicable defence was that there was no real malice and intent to murder, so manslaughter would seem to be apposite. Smith had to rely, as every lawyer did then, on the M'Naghten Rules, stating that if insanity is proven there is an absence of a mens rea, an intent to kill, and so the jury should commit the prisoner to hospital and confinement for an indefinite period. For Smith, his only basis for argument was the instance of the 'fits'. The M'Naghten Rules had been laid down as recently as 1844 and the crucially important words were 'the accused . . . at the time of committing the act, must have been labouring under such defect of reason, from disease of the mind, as not to know the nature and quality of the act'. The formative event here was the murder of Sir Robert Peel's private secretary by Daniel M'Naghten, who was tried in 1843; the proceedings were halted over a plea of insanity.

In the first decades of the nineteenth century there was a steady realisation that the new science of psychiatry could play a part in the understanding and sentencing of crime. The issue of who was bad and who was mad had become, by the 1850s, something that demanded debate. A number of medical men working in asylums or in universities began to identify varieties of insanity and distinguish them from such behaviour as epileptic fits. None of this knowledge would be applied in this case of murder in a remote part of Lincolnshire.

This was because Huddleston saw no problem at all with Drant's behaviour and general condition. His words were, 'The law presumed all killing to be murder and it rested upon the accused to show that the offence was manslaughter only.' Amazingly, he spoke directly to the jury in his summing up and directed them not to take 'a cowardly refuge in either alternative [manslaughter or insanity] to avoid responsibility'. To be fair, he instructed them with reference to the M'Naghten Rules but then led the summary into a recounting of the accused's actions on the fateful day.

Drant, he reminded them, had been subject to no provocation from Gell in terms of an attempt to stop him injuring his mother. He did admit that Drant had had a violent blow to the back of his head, and that 'this had confused him' and rather unexpectedly opened up the possibility of an escape from the murder charge: 'The accused snatched up the first weapon near him and so caused the death of the deceased . . . the offence might be manslaughter.' The jury took twenty-five minutes to decide that Drant was guilty of murder.

On 7 December a major figure in the new psychology of deviance wrote a letter to *The Times* about the case. This was Henry Maudsley, a man who was totally preoccupied with the debate on what was then called 'degeneration' – an off-shoot of Darwinian evolution – which was concerned wth understanding criminality in terms of genetic and physiological traits. Maudsley was interested in the epilepsy alleged to be in Drant's medical profile. Maudsley drew attention to the condition of Drant before the onset of the violence: 'On the evening of the murder he had been taken ill in a neighbour's cottage; he was cold, trembled very much and was extremely pale in the face, crying out, "Oh Lord save me!"' Maudsley had reflected on the progress of the outburst, read between the lines, and seen a familiar pattern of epileptic symptoms. Arguably, informed public opinion must have been affected by such a prominent medical man writing to *The Times* about the affair. His lengthy, detailed letter, expressed with care and precision, must have alarmed the legal professionals who had experienced such behaviour in previous cases. That such a respected doctor even noticed an obscure killing in rural Lincolnshire was also notably rare.

Maudsley then noted that the most useful information about the illness came from Drant's mother. She had said that her son had had fits since he was a child, and that he had two such seizures on the Tuesday before the killing, and 'four or five' again on the Wednesday. She went on, 'He usually went violent after these fits. During the time he was in the house on the fateful night he was talking to himself. I washed him about seven o'clock when he was trembling violently and seemed to know nothing.' Quite rightly, Maudsley was acute enough to realise that the person closest to the killer, his mother, was well informed about the 'case history' and in fact expressed the symptoms and habits of the poor victim of the illness very ably and accurately. Once again, we have a Victorian murder trial in which the medical discourse available is very limited and mostly unheard.

Mrs Drant said that the local doctor, Boulton, had attended William several times recently, and that a few days before the incident she had slept with her bedroom door open for fear of her son's likely sudden fit of rage or distraction. All this was just what Maudsley needed to confirm an opinion that should have found a place in the trial: he wrote that such behaviour was 'epileptic mania . . . is well known to have most furious and dangerous consequences'. His description of the condition certainly fits Drant's case: he was described as 'Sane enough, perhaps, and even amiable, industrious and well-behaved during their fits, then these unfortunate persons become immediately after them most violent and destructive beings for a time . . . and when they come to themselves they are utterly unconscious of what they have done in their state of alienation.' The doctor had seen the significance of the pattern of Drant's actions and suffering, and seen them as a template, a defining sequence of manifestations of the illness.

Perhaps Maudsley caught the real mood of the Hemingby people after the trial, because he put on his academic tone and said that if a lecturer were to be given a case study of Drant he would not be able to quote 'a more typical example than the painful case of William Drant who is now lying under sentence of death'. Drant's neighbours and fellow citizens petitioned the Home Office asking for a reprieve, and it was granted. He was detained 'during Her Majesty's pleasure'.

It was *The Times* court reporter who had called this 'a painful case', and it is a fitting description. As for the victim, Constable Gell, he was buried in the churchyard at Hemingby, surely respected and admired by his friends and clients.

Maudsley, who had played a part in helping the case to this conclusion, went on to found a centre for research into mental illness, a happy departure from the normal practice of setting up yet another asylum. Ironically, only a short distance from Hemingby, the Lincoln Bracebridge Asylum had by 1890 almost a thousand patients inside its walls. Sadly for Drant, there is no doubt that he faced a future in which his epileptic attacks would take place in very

The Assize judge arrives. Lincoln was famous for its excellent accommodation for judges and lawyers. (Author's Collection)

unpleasant circumstances, and with no medical men with the understanding of Maudsley in attendance.

The new policing was slow to spread across the country. J.J. Tobias has written in his *Crime and Industrial Society in the Nineteenth Century*: ' . . . even when the new police was extended to England and Wales and a new professionalism imparted by the appointment of Her Majesty's Inspectors of Constabulary, it was several years before the whole country was efficiently policed'. There was a widespread suspicion of the new police, which helped delay their spread. As many historians of the period have argued, the radical populace viewed any police as a political, not a protective, force. Some free-thinkers even argued that they were really soldiers under another name. Memories of the Peterloo Massacre were passed down and not forgotten.

The only real complaints the locals had made about unacceptable criminal behaviour in Hemingby up to this time, and during the regime of the constables in the years before the county police, were about the regular disturbance of people playing skittles and gaming in Hemingby Lane. To find they were now in a village in which a police officer had been murdered must have been very unpleasant, and many must surely then have welcomed the new 'professionals'.

Drant's story was just one of many which slowly brought about some changes in the relationship between the courts and their professionals, and the medical men who were increasingly called upon to pass informed opinions. Even so the place of epilepsy, as a part of a defence in court, continued to be problematical well into the twentieth century. Some homicide cases between the wars involved discussions as to whether or not 'petit mal' constitutes extenuating circumstances with regard to a defence case.

There had been other deaths besides Gell's in the line of duty in the new police; only three years before this murder PC Tidbury had received a medal for gallantry for jumping from a moving train to recapture a prisoner. Two years after the Horncastle drama PC Little had rescued a lady 'from a most perilous position' on a rooftop. The Albert Medal was created in 1866, and preceded what was to become the King's Police Medal of 1909. Unfortunately there was no such award for Gell; there will never be anything 'heroic' about running across town and meeting a crazed man in a homicidal fit.

7

THE WIFE KILLER

I, George J. Michison, surgeon of Her Majesty's Prison of Lincoln, hereby certify that I this day examined the body of Joseph Bowser, on whom judgement of death was this day executed in the said prison, and that on examination I found that the said Joseph Bowser was dead.

Dated this 27th day of July, 1897

George Michison

This brief official statement tells the end of a life which the victim was happy and prepared to lose. To reach that dark place of the soul he had killed, and with malice. This murder is one of the most callous in Lincolnshire records.

In the years between 1890 and 1901 the area around Holbeach and Spalding had a series of terrible murders, all in rural communities, and many were savage in the extreme. The horrendous decade began with a mother killing her two children, and then herself, not far from Spalding; at the end of the period, in June 1901, a wife was shot by her husband and the man then cut his throat. It is tempting to ask what was in the air, or what particular social factors were affecting the well-being and harmony of these remote communities. As it was an age before sociology and studies of the effects of debt and unemployment we can only speculate about the probable causes.

But one open and callous murder stands out in that period: a man shooting his wife as she looked boldly into the barrel of his gun, knowing that her fate was imminent. This happened at Donington Northorpe, a market town between Spalding and Boston that was once important in the hemp and flax production in the county. The area is rightly called 'wet fen', and there was a salt water fen there for many years until banking was done to keep out the sea. Its most famous son is surely the adventurer Matthew Flinders; its most infamous is arguably Joseph Bowser, killer of his wife at their home in 1897.

This man was overseer of the poor and guardian of the Spalding Union, clearly a man with respect attached to his name, and something of a good local reputation. He was a farmer with a wife who had been married before. She started as his housekeeper, being known to all as Mrs Harrison, but became Mrs Bowser in 1886 and apparently had a happy married life for some time, or so witnesses were to testify later when the man was in the dock at Lincoln. Their relationship seemed good to those who knew them superficially, but there were undoubtedly problems with Susan, the wife. On one occasion, after a rough quarrel, she convinced Joseph she had taken poison and a doctor was rushed out to attend to her. However, it was all a ruse, a deception to achieve something that would, of course, only serve to exacerbate their already rocky emotional relationship.

Other things were stirring deep down in Bowser's complicated nature, and on the morning of 25 May he indulged his liking for a drinking session by staying in bed, nursing a bottle of whisky. Susan merely carried on with the household chores. She had a servant girl called Berridge. Friends called around to pay a visit: one, Fred Lister, was shortly to emigrate to South Africa; the other, Eliza Drury, was from Wyberton Chain Bridge. Everyone except Joseph enjoyed a sociable lunch, and the visitors went for a walk. In the afternoon Bowser decided to stir and he came downstairs as Susan was mixing some chicken food and acting quite normally.

Whatever had been brewing in his sour, drunken mind now came to fruition, and in a nasty outburst he asked what she was doing. She simply said it was food for the chickens, whereupon Joseph made his first attack. He kicked her, and it seems astonishing that Susan only said, 'Don't do that' (according to the servant) and walked outside to the Home Field area to feed the birds. The drunken man followed and began to kick her again; a fury was on him now, and the drink had him in a mad passion. So severe was the beating he gave his wife that she lay unable to move. He then walked back inside the house.

The statement 'Don't do that' is puzzling for the crime historian. Does it imply a long-standing acceptance on the wife's part of the violent man she had to live with? It is so mild that it invites us to consider that she may have tolerated too much for too long. Or, was this highly unusual behaviour on the part of her killer? There is too little in her puzzling reactions to the initial vicious attack to help us decide.

It is hard to imagine what Lister must have thought when Joseph appeared, clearly intoxicated, and asked if he had any cartridges. Bowser had taken his double-barrelled gun from a hook in the kitchen. The report in the *Lincolnshire Chronicle* stated that Bowser said, 'I'll fetch one out of the room – she'll not aggravate me any more.' He was busy readying himself for something horrendous, and there was a sense of impending drama in the place.

At that point the servant did something amazingly brave and admirable: she went outside, fearing the worst was about to happen to her mistress, and tried to move her out of harm's way, but Susan Bowser was too injured to move. The attack had done some severe damage to her spine. She knew what was coming and said, 'Let him shoot' to the servant. The girl's narrative of the events implies that Susan was a formidable and strong personality, and she prepared herself stoically for the assault as she lay helpless on the ground.

The girl would not move from Susan's side, and both women stared at Bowser as he came out with the gun, ready to shoot. Apparently Susan stared him straight in the face and seemed without emotion. The two women held hands. We have to wonder where Lister was at this juncture. He must have suspected something fairly nasty was about to happen. Bowser was reckless and determined and pulled the trigger. The drink in him affected his accuracy and the cartridge cracked into the wooden wall of the calf-house. The women were still looking at him, like two people facing a firing squad, apparently resigned and helpless.

Bowser fired again, and this time, as the official report put it, 'the woman fell, her brains bespattering the door at her rear; the shot having entered her head immediately above the right eye'. Walking back inside, he coolly reported what he had done to the visitors. These two went out to verify what he claimed he had done; as for Bowser, he was sober enough to request that Lister contact his two brothers, and then he sat resignedly and waited for the police and the doctor. Other neighbours had arrived on the scene by the time the law arrived, and Bowser was heard to say, 'They have come for me; there is the gun I did it with . . . I expect I shall be hung for this.'

His simple words could not have been more accurate. Seldom had a court had a more straightforward, uncomplicated case to consider. At the Lincoln Assizes, Baron Pollock was in charge, and the statements of the witnesses, together with Bowser's own confession and the lack of any required defence makes it seem likely, figuratively speaking, that Pollock had the black cap ready to hand under his desk from the moment the trial started. Baron Pollock was a notable writer as well as a judge in high esteem. He had come to the bar in 1871 and was Professor of Jurisprudence at Oxford at this time. He was the man who was to fix Oscar Wilde's bail at £4,000 not long after his visit to Lincoln.

The Bowser case was one of several cases he tried. When he was younger, only three years into his legal career, he had presided over another drunken murder of a wife. John Eblethrift had stabbed his wife to death, but at the time he had thought she had a lover hidden in the house. In that case, Pollock had been willing to agree to a manslaughter charge, but this did not happen in Bowser's. What lay behind this judicial inconsistency was the idea of a 'reasonable man' and how that imaginary figure would behave. A reasonable man would not, like Bowser, drink a bottle of whisky and brood until he crossed over into unacceptable behaviour. The fact that the alcohol would have caused chemical changes in his brain was a concept well beyond medical knowledge then.

If we take a wider view of what actually happened in that Lincoln Assizes with Bowser in the dock, we can see that it was one drama in a long series of debates about what constituted provocation and what was 'insanity' in the view of the law. In a murder trial ten years before this Lincolnshire one, in which a drunken husband had killed his wife, the judge saw a 'drunken intent to kill' as not different from a reasoned, sober intent. But throughout the nineteenth century judges and juries did not always see distinctions regarding insane acts and drunken acts in the same way. An example of just how much a good lawyer could influence things was in a case in 1880, again involving a drunken husband stabbing his wife to death. His lawyer said that this was a case of temporary insanity. The term was extremely contentious at the time.

Reading between the lines, it is possible to envisage that there were difficulties between the couple after ten years of marriage: something was rankling in Bowser's mind, and drink was the trigger to action. It is useless to speculate what exactly happened to drive him to murder. Was there an aim to her ruse about taking her own life? Was her mental health a factor? Alas, it must all remain a mystery. There are thousands of instances in the Victorian and Edwardian periods of wife-murder or assault that tell a tale of brutality tolerated for years, and no-one in the neighbourhood knowing anything about the situation until either 'the worm turned' or the bullying went too far and became public knowledge and a disgrace. Naturally, this all becomes more complex as we try to appraise the issues through modern eyes. Commentators at that time did not have a discourse of 'battered wife syndrome' to apply.

But for Joseph Bowser, the issue of to what extent Susan had provoked him to kill was never considered. It may well have been that she had had a lover (in the past or in the present). According to one researcher, the outcome of all this courtroom uncertainty about what constituted provocation was that in cases of a spouse murdering a spouse in the 1880s and '90s, the number of jury verdicts expressed as 'unfit to plead' or plain 'insane' doubled.

The local papers took a pride in reporting Bowser's last hours on earth, and cashed in on the Victorian public's hunger for information about executions. They reported on the 'callousness and indifference that were part of his gross nature' and made a point of stressing that he had added a stone and a half to his weight since he was imprisoned at Greetwell Road. He rose early, saw the chaplain at 8 a.m., and then went for his appointment with the Lancashire hangman, James Billington, and his son, who had stayed in the prison the previous night after a long journey south. No doubt the increase in bulk made his exit easier.

There were the two familiar communications across the city at 8.45 a.m.: the black flag raised and the peeling of Big Tom, the bell at Lincoln Cathedral. Eardley Wilmot, the prison governor, with John Bond, the chaplain, confirmed that the judgment of death had been carried out, and in the correct manner. Just as Bowser had been firm in his resolve to take a life, so he was in control and collected when he walked to the scaffold. The local reporter had an unhealthy interest in finding out some details for his report, noting, 'From inquiries we learn that the culprit bore himself with great firmness. It was only at two minutes to nine that the executioner and his assistant entered the pinioning room, and proceeded with their operations, which were accomplished with marvellous celerity.'

Bowser at the time of his death weighed 17 stone, and, as Lincoln had been the place where local hangman William Marwood had perfected his 'long drop' (a humane method of hanging criminals) a short while before this, it was with relish that the reporter gave details of 'a drop of only 4 feet 6 inches'. Marwood, from Horncastle, had been something of a celebrity and notorious beyond Lincolnshire for his pride in his profession. He was in the habit of coming into Lincoln the night before a hanging to enjoy a few drinks at his favourite inns, The Strugglers and the White Hart, and then to take time to do thorough preparations for the work at the scaffold. His basic arithmetic about the ratio of weight and length of rope was impressive. Marwood died in 1883, and his successor James Berry retired in 1891. Therefore James Billington hanged Bowser: capable, but not a perfectionist. Bowser wanted his life to end, and quickly. He had his wish. Great Tom, the bell, chimed.

The executioner William Marwood (1820–83), who perfected the 'long drop'. He took his work seriously and liked the media attention that his job created. (Author's Collection)

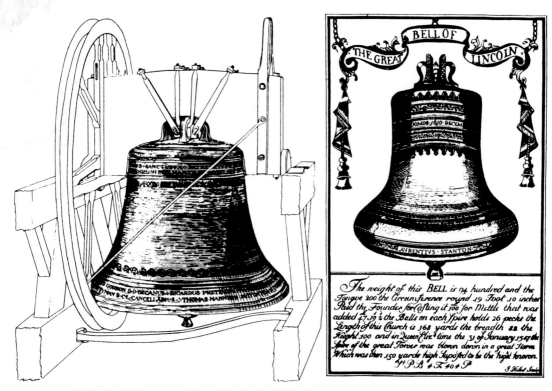

Great Tom, the bell tolled at executions. (Author's Collection)

The coroner's jury took a last look at Bowser's body before he was buried and quicklimed, with lime produced on a site next door to the prison. The mechanics of state execution in that period were efficient and planned with military precision – much as Bowser's murder of his wife was. Commentators on the decline of society at the time, full of talk about the awful degeneration of the 'lower orders', saw in this type of domestic killing a confirmation that debilitating idleness and drink were ruining the workers. They saw the sharp rise in wife-murder in the 1890s as a sign of a general malaise. But most of these same writers would not have approved of the barbarous way the state punished the killers.

8

A CRIME OF PASSION

The number of casualties in the First World War was massive; the statistics of the dead are horrendous to contemplate. But many victims of that war died long after the Armistice of mental, not physical wounds. In that horrific conflict deserters had been shot and condemned as cowards; men with mental illness had been largely misunderstood; and many of the worst casualties were 'walking wounded' long after they put down their rifles for the last time. This is a dramatic account of the fate of one such casualty, which was played out in a quiet village where nothing usually disturbed the silence apart from the lowing of cattle.

Fulbeck, between Grantham and Lincoln, was described by one writer of guide books in 1926 as 'a very pretty village . . . with charming old houses, grey and red'. The guide did not mention what had happened there just seven years before it came into print: the savage murder of teenager Florence Jackson by George Rowland. Here was a murder case that would open up many of the tangled rules and statements about insanity that had caused problems for judges and juries for many decades.

George Rowland was eleven years older than Florence, and when he thought she had another man he could not cope with the feelings this caused in him. He lived in Grantham and she in Fulbeck, to the north, and in his visits to her he became increasingly possessive and controlling. On 31 May 1919 they went to the feast at nearby Caythorpe and Florence went to enjoy herself on a swingboat ride. Unfortunately for her, she spent time with another young man on that ride. This increased Rowland's jealous state. He had fought in the First World War and, like many young men in that terrible conflict, had been gassed and suffered a number of wounds. All was not well with his mental state.

They walked home and stopped by a place called Gascoyne's Gate near a Fulbeck brickyard. Richard Snelson, who was walking by the place a little later, met Rowland, who was bleeding, and heard his story of how a young woman had tried to attack him and then taken her own life. Snelson followed Rowland to the spot where Florence now lay, and saw a young woman with her throat cut, a razor in her hand and indications that she had been involved in a fight. Florence's sister, Laura, passed while walking home from the feast, and Rowland confessed to her he had 'killed her Flo'. He mentioned that it was because she had been with another man. This was late at night, after ten o'clock. The murder had taken place just 150 yards from the houses at the edge of the village. Laura fetched her mother; she attacked Rowland, and had to be restrained. She raged, 'They would not let me kill him!'

His trial at Crown Court took place on 3 November, with Justice Greer sitting to hear the charge of murder. The defence, led by a Mr Wright, declared they would present a story of insanity, with roots in the young man's war experience. Accordingly, at the swearing-in of the jury, it was stated that their priority was to decide whether or not Rowland was 'of sound mind'. The medical expert called to testify was Dr Alfred Ewan, superintendent of the Kesteven County Asylum. This doctor, with decades of experience of work with mental patients behind him, stated that he did not consider Rowland to be fit to be tried. He had attended Rowland on several occasions before this tragic event. He said that he was of the opinion that 'he is not in such a mental condition that he can take his trial'. The judge told him that it was not his opinion that counted but that of the jury. Here again was another instance of the complications surrounding the insanity defence.

The illiterate young man, whose father had called him 'dull', was then described by the medical man as someone who had always had a 'simple' mind, and was so childish that he did not understand what was happening. His actual words were, 'From what I have learned of him from his youth upwards he has never been of a normal mental standard.' Greer asked the doctor to confirm that the prisoner would not be able to comprehend a simple question regarding the action of murder, and therefore would not be aware of the notion of 'intention'. Ewan replied that that was perhaps not really the case but that Rowland 'frequently contradicted himself'.

What emerged was a scenario typical of hundreds of such trials: despite being told that the doctor thought Rowland had the mind of a boy of twelve, the jury thought the young man fit to stand trial.

Naturally some account of the man's military experience was demanded. It was explained that Rowland had joined the British Expeditionary Force (BEF) on 6 April 1915 and had been wounded in combat; when he left the army in 1919 he took a job at Ruston and Hornby in Grantham. His army record was commendable. Not long after, on his strolls around the villages looking for entertainment, Rowland met Florence. Her mother had not liked the man's obvious wish to influence and control her daughter's life, but Florence had insisted that she could handle him. Then in late May he went to stay with the Jacksons. What he took with him included a razor, strop and brush, along with the obligatory toothbrush. (The razor was a commonly used murder weapon in any number of cases between the First World War and the 1930s; it occurs in all kinds of places and cases.)

At the fair Florence had joined a man called Edward Knights on the swingboats. Knights and Rowland then drank together at the Red Lion pub and at that time Rowland asked if he had been courting his girl, Florence. Although Knights said that he had not, Rowland had not believed him. Knights's account of the evening suggested a certain degree of distraction and irrational speech from Rowland, who asked him if he had been a sergeant in the Flying Corps. He appeared to interrogate Knights, looking for some information, before walking home with Florence. From somewhere he had got the notion that the girl had been 'keeping company with someone from the Flying Corps', which would cast doubt on her moral behaviour, such was the reputation of the new flyers. The truth was surely that young Florence wanted to have some fun, but was stuck with this serious young man with a deeply troubled nature and a profoundly disturbed interior life as a result of horrendous battlefield stress.

Reflection about the encounter with the other young man at the fair and the inquisition about his being in the Flying Corps indicate the kind of irrational fixation that can be part of a depressive illness: to be viewing a situation in such a distorted way surely hints at a boyish, immature nature and a strong sense of insecurity. It has echoes of a playground challenge and a wish to assert some kind of impetuous superiority.

Knights's account of the meeting with Rowland suggests that the ex-soldier was indeed deeply troubled; he challenged Knights to fight with fists or guns but Knights refused. The couple then walked home by way of the track to Fulbeck in the dark spring evening.

The witness, Snelson, stated he was walking on the Fulbeck track when Rowland approached him and said, 'Eh, chummy, stop! Fetch a motor car, quick. There has been a nasty accident,' and told him the tale of the attempted suicide. However, it was established in court that the gash to Florence's throat was definitely not done by her own hand. The words Rowland used are strangely innocuous and inappropriate in a report of such a brutal act.

Florence's sister Laura then had to recount her experience of that dreadful night. She said that the only explanation Rowland had given her was, 'Another man wanted her. I have tried to kill myself, but could not.' He told a different story to a couple called Greensmith, who also saw the body. Rowland said he 'had a job on' – the colloquial way of indicating that there was an insuperable task ahead, or that there was an element of impossibility in what he had set himself. When Greensmith asked how the girl had died, Rowland answered, 'It's like this. She tried to kill me, but she could not, and so she killed herself . . . look, the razor is in her hand.'

To Florence's mother, when she arrived, Rowland said that he had killed his 'darling', and he repeated the ridiculous account of the girl attacking him to the first constable who came on the scene. There was never any subterfuge.

The judge's lodgings, Castle Square. The grand and impressive lodgings are still used today. (Author's Collection)

Rowland's father was the only one who touched on his war experience with any telling effect: he said that his son had always been dull but had been 'a lot worse after the war'. Today, Rowland's condition would be recognised as post-traumatic stress syndrome and treated accordingly. But in 1919 even Mr Rowland's account of his having to sit up all night with his son as the boy shouted, 'Jerry's over the top, they're coming!' does not seem to have had much effect in court; nor did the fact that he had been gassed in the war. However, the jury did, despite finding Rowland guilty, recommend mercy. The black cap had to be put on Greer's head and the sentence passed, but the next step was the court of appeal on 24 November. At least Rowland's case, unlike those of some other men who killed after fighting in the war and undergoing transmutations of personality, would be re-examined.

Serving in the BEF had meant Rowland was one of 100,000 fresh recruits involved in a war in which machine guns could deal out death to hundreds in seconds and trench warfare meant trying to run across fields of mud against a storm of bullets. The man who could come home from that without mental scars of some kind would be rare indeed. In Rowland's case there was no real medical help, just a father who sat with him and talked him out of his nightmares. With hindsight, the situation at the time with regard to what we now call post-traumatic stress syndrome was complex in the extreme, and

COMMITTEE ON INSANITY AND CRIME,

REPORT

OF THE

Committee appointed to consider what changes, if any, are desirable in the existing law, practice and procedure relating to criminal trials in which the plea of insanity as a defence is raised, and whether any and, if so, what changes should be made in the existing law and practice in respect of cases falling within the provisions of section 2 (4) of the Criminal Lunatics Act, 1884,

Presented to Parliament by Command of His Majesty.

LONDON:
PRINTED & PUBLISHED BY HIS MAJESTY'S STATIONERY OFFICE.
To be purchased directly from H.M. STATIONERY OFFICE at the following addresses:
Imperial House, Kingsway, London, W.C.2; 28, Abingdon Street, London, S.W.1;
York Street, Manchester; 1, St. Andrew's Crescent, Cardiff;
or 120, George Street, Edinburgh;
or through any Bookseller.

1924

Price 6d. net.

Cmd. 2005.

Report on Insanity and Crime, *1924, one of the many documents testifying to the attempts to understand insanity within the criminal law.* (Author's Collection) mixed with all kinds of expressions of patriotism and the current masculine ethos. If we ask what help Rowland would have had in terms of some therapy for his mind, the answer is very little. So many cases of neurasthenia were complicated by the resolute insistence of the sufferers on being stoical and maintaining the instilled discipline of their training, thereby subverting attempts to treat them with psychotherapy.

The BEF had so much experience of confined area shell attack that a psychiatrist was brought in, but he never had more than an advisory or experimental role. When an application was put to the Home Secretary for a reprieve for Rowland, the stark, disturbing facts of the effects of shell-shock were becoming well known, the effects felt by the men mostly being mutism and nervous exhaustion. At first the thinking was that these illnesses were caused by the changes in pressure as bombs fell in confined areas, but after the bloodbath of the Somme in 1916 the view changed somewhat. Unfortunately the only therapies available were simple rest cure or electro-convulsive treatment.

Rowland had been one of the men recalled to action within a month of the first shell-shock trauma, one of 87,000 men in that condition. Back home, when there was some attempt at treatment, it was limited, and it was further complicated by a sense of shame: as one nurse recalled, 'There was a great shame in shell-shock and men just kept repeating that they couldn't help their nerves.' Rowland's nightmares and repression of emotion, as noted by his father, are relevant here. The war poet, Wilfred Owen, talks about 'morbid, terrifying slumber'.

Finally, perhaps as a result of general discussion of these factors, and an awareness of just how numerous were the crimes involving ex-soldiers with 'neurasthenia' as it was called, there was a brief announcement in *The Times* of 2 December 1919:

DEATH SENTENCE RESPITED
The Home Secretary has advised the King to respite the death sentence passed on George Richard Rowland at Lincoln Assizes with a view to commutation to penal servitude for life. Rowland was found guilty of murdering Florence Jackson on the way home from a village feast at Fulbeck, Lincolnshire.

A respite meant a reprieve, not a pardon. That can only mean that there was a consideration that Rowland was insane. The law at the time stated that 'in the case of capital offences it is his [the magistrate's] duty thus to respite the sentence if the prisoner be proved to be insane'. The Royal Committee on Insanity and Crime was to issue a report in 1924, long after the new knowledge of trench warfare, in which it dictated that 'accused persons should not be found on arraignment unfit to plead except on the evidence of at least two doctors, save in very clear cases'. That report contains a great deal that had been learned too late, with some remorse in the hindsight, about the kinds of trauma the First World War inflicted. Between the wars, in the north-east for instance, a large proportion of domestic murders (usually where a man killed his wife or girlfriend) were carried out by war veterans, and statements about their mental health were still being expressed in amateurish discourse, even by medical men.

Maybe the Home Secretary was made aware that at the Assizes things had been rather rushed and the insanity issue never really applied to the trauma of the young man's war wounds and shell-shock. After all, some time needed to pass before a fuller understanding of war experience could emerge. We now know much more about this, and we know that psychiatric casualties have to be immediately removed from the front to base hospitals. Combat fatigue must be treated quickly after being observed and described.

FARMHOUSE SHOOTINGS: TEENAGER AND DOG?

Waddingham and Gedney, 1931

This is a shocking story of something that took place in a village now perhaps best known for a best-selling countryside memoir, *Hedingham Harvest* by Geoffrey Robinson, published in 1977. This was arguably Lincolnshire's answer to the idyll of Laurie Lee's *Cider with Rosie*, but there was nothing idyllic about the events in the real village fictionalised as Hedingham. In a place where the normal sounds were those of harvesting machines and tractors, there were gunshots in 1931. Even today Waddingham is a tranquil place, well away from the main roads that run up the spine of the county, between the Lincolnshire Wolds and the Lindsey farmland down the escarpment ridge by the Roman road south to Lincoln. It is very hard to imagine tragic events taking place in this rural calm but they did, and the consequences were to have national importance.

In 1844 *The Times* reported an item in its court reports that was highly unusual. The wording reads strangely today, almost as if the writer was trying to come to terms with something exceptional even in the tough and unfeeling world of Victorian criminal law. There had been two murders in Boston, Lincolnshire, and they were committed by a girl of thirteen.

MURDERS BY A YOUNG CHILD

On Monday evening last was committed to Lincoln Castle for trial at the ensuing assizes, charged with the wilful murder of her two little brothers, Mary Johnson . . . it has proved one of the most pitiable and painful and intricate investigations which have occurred in this part of the country for many years.

In 1931 Lincolnshire again had a case that could be described as 'pitiable, painful and intricate', and the killer was a teenager. Even more shocking was that this killing happened in the beautiful village of Waddingham, between

Scunthorpe and Louth. The rural calm of this tranquil spot was to be shaken, and the story covered the national papers' main crime reports for some time. The echoes of the case were far-reaching, having an impact on the Report on Capital Punishment put together in 1957. A nephew shot his aunt and uncle as they lay in bed. In a context in which guns were always lying around, ready for use in hunting and shooting pigeons and rats, there was always a risk, but no-one expected a child to pick one up and deal out death, and certainly not to his own kin.

The killings had been horrific. Anne and Robert Jacklin were found dead in their beds by Robert's father, who visited one morning. He had to force his way in after getting no response to his shouts and found himself faced by a fire smouldering downstairs, where some hay had been lit. He then heard the cries of his grandchild upstairs. In the parents' bedroom he found the body of his daughter-in-law and then his son, still alive but bleeding profusely on the floor by the bed. In the corner of the room the couple's baby lay unharmed. Harold Smith, the couple's nephew, slept in an adjoining room, but Mr Jacklin found the room empty that morning, as he confirmed in court.

Robert survived for two days before dying in Lincoln County Hospital. His upper jaw and nose had been shot away. His only recorded account of the incident as he lay dying in agony was that he had opened his eyes to find his wife covered in blood, and that he had no explanation of what had taken place in his lonely farmhouse. What had been ascertained at the time, after James Jacklin had called in Superintendent Dalby from Brigg, was reported in the *Lincolnshire Chronicle* with an emphasis on the drama: 'The bedroom window was open and there was a trail of blood to the window sill as though the injured man had struggled to the window to call for aid. But a call from the lonely spot, nearly one and a half miles from the nearest neighbour, was not likely to be of much avail.' The unfortunate father who had walked in on this scene of blood and suffering was to prove an accurate observer: his testimony suggested a certain pattern of actions and repercussions, although his emotional condition must have been extremely delicate and frantic as he tried to come to terms with the bloodbath in the farm building.

Harold Smith, just sixteen, told two stories. The first was that he had decided, after simply not being able to 'get on' with his aunt and uncle (who employed him), that he had had enough and was going to shoot them. He said that he picked up a shotgun and stood at their bedroom door for a while, debating whether or not to kill them. He knew they were both in bed. 'I got out of bed about quarter past four, got the shotgun and stood outside the bedroom for four or five minutes,' he said. His second statement said that his uncle Robert had shot his aunt and then turned the gun on himself. A medical expert confirmed that the suicide of Robert Jacklin was quite plausible, as the wounds were consistent with a shot fired from close range. This seemed to some at the time like a very bizarre theory. A strange account of events was put to the jury, one which said that Jacklin had woken, seen his wife dead, and then, in sheer despair, found a gun and shot himself through the jaw. The whole idea appears to be ridiculous.

Harold comes across in the trial report as a young man with severe problems in expressing himself and an inability to communicate fine distinctions in meaning and feeling; today we might apply such terms as Asperger's syndrome but there is no evidence to suggest that kind of extreme condition. It is more likely that he was treated like a skivvy and so became insensitive in the worst degree, and his lack of meaningful human communication gradually eroded his sense of worth and belonging. With this being a likely pattern of life for him, some elements of his awful crime are understandable, but only to a limited extent.

The focus returned to the first statement by the boy, in which he had said, 'At last I touched the trigger and the gun went off and it shot Mr Jacklin. Then Mrs Jacklin looked up and I shot her as well.' Mr E.W. Cave, for the prosecution, read this and knew he had a solid case. James Jacklin, the 71-year-old father of Robert, stated that he found two spent cartridges in the bedroom and later found the gun outside in the coal house.

When questioned in court, Smith made things even more complicated by saying he had not used the gun and that his muttered confession to the shooting originally was, 'I thought it would help me through it', and that he had been apprehensive against the forces of authority: 'I did not think that my word would be believed against so many.'

So who shot the husband? Nothing is clear on this point. All that was to happen related solely to the murder of Anne Jacklin, and the finger pointed to young Harold Smith. He was found guilty of murder but with a strong recommendation for mercy. But the death sentence was passed, and newsmen reported that the young man 'remained calm and showed no traces of emotion'. Journalists went away to search for facts about the last hangings of teenagers, and there was much contemporary coverage of five people of eighteen years of age who had been executed in Britain since 1885. There were obviously protracted discussions in the press about the need for the reform of the criminal law on this matter. There was talk of William Calcraft, the legendary hangman.

The Home Secretary, Sir Herbert Samuel, received an appeal; popular opinion insisted that the whole matter needed clearing up, and that Samuel was the man to do it. One of the prominent lawyers in the debate expressed the dilemma in this way: 'I am sure that public opinion cannot approve of the death sentence being passed on boys of this tender age when there is no likelihood of it being carried into effect.'

The sentence was commuted to penal servitude. This sentence had been introduced into the criminal justice system as long ago as 1853, as it was being realised just how expensive transportation to Australia was – and also

William Calcraft (1800–79) supervised hundreds of executions. (Laura Carter)

how perilous the journey was to the health of convicts. Smith was destined to be sewing mailbags for the rest of his life.

The tale is surely an important milestone in the long and contentious development of more humane sentencing in the British penal system, and also testifies to the still largely static nature of ideas about criminal justice in the inter-war years. That is the essential outline of this murder narrative, but now we must look more closely at it.

There is a long and complex prelude to this case. Young Smith had been working for his aunt and uncle at Holme Farm since the previous January. The murder took place on 3 October. His relationship with his parents was uncertain and troubled. They lived in the village of Scawby, about 10 miles away towards Brigg, and had wanted him to do a proper job of work, bringing in some income. The boy had hated life at Holme Farm and had once tried to run away, but had been found and taken back to work by his father. There is much more meaning behind his statement, 'We have not been comfortable', with reference to his victims than was discussed in court.

It must be said that there is a hidden element in the Smith case: the role and attitudes of his own family in events. This notable omission suggests that there was much more to the family situation at Scawby than ever reached the written records. Today words like 'neglect' might be used, or even discussion around the theme of 'excluded groups' in society. But although little is known of Smith's home life, we do know that in the 1930s it was common practice in many parts of the land to send children away to work in branches of the family, particularly when families had many children, and strenuous efforts were made to keep work within the extended family network. Smith was a victim of this practice. Also at least some of his rebelliousness can be attributed to teenage revolt and dissatisfaction, but of course there was no place for that in the courtroom of 1931.

Harold Smith was certainly a 'tearaway' and a problem to his parents, but their treatment was not exactly sensitive by modern standards. At that time hard physical labour was still considered to be something akin to 'character forming' for young people. But the boy could not bear the demands of his relatives in that isolated place. When James Jacklin arrived on the day of the murder, Robert's bicycle was missing, and so was Harold. The killer had taken off into the lanes of Lincolnshire, terrified at what he had done on a moment's impulse. But in legal terms, the fact that he had been hostile towards the couple for some time, when added to his tale about waiting by the door with the loaded gun, contemplating taking the two adults' lives, clearly made this a murder case.

Smith was sentenced on 6 October, but it did not take long for the reprieve to be considered. Sir Herbert Samuel had only just been appointed to the Cabinet as the new Home Secretary. Almost his first task must have been to respond to the call for leniency. According to the criminal law in 1931, anyone under the age of sixteen could not be tried for murder, and Smith was just a few months over. The last Home Secretary, J.R. Clynes, Labour, was asked to comment and he insisted that there was an urgent need for reform on the issue. He expressed it with an uncommon humanity for the moral attitudes of the time: 'I am sure that public opinion cannot approve of the death sentence being passed on boys of this tender age when there is no likelihood of it being carried into effect.' But before Samuel set to work, the poor boy had to stand in the dock while the black cap was put on. The local reports stressed his fortitude: 'He stood stiffly in the dock while the judge . . . pronounced the dread words of the formal sentence, "and may the Lord have mercy on your soul".'

Harold Smith's reprieve was approved the day after the trial, 7 October. There had been no real doubt in Samuel's mind about his decision. The pressure of both public opinion and of the professionals within the process of the criminal law was too strong to resist. This is to say nothing of another relevant factor: that Samuel knew what a boost this would be for his new public image, in office and immediately on the main pages of the dailies.

When one of the most radical reforms of policy on capital punishment took place after the 1957 report, the recommendation on the issue of executing teenage killers was partly a result of the Smith case; an act in 1933, the Children and Young Persons Act, had tackled the 'under eighteen' watershed, as had an act of 1908, but it had not fully resolved the problem. Clearly, the reason for some persistent doubts was that each homicide case has its own specific features, and questions of sanity/insanity or what constitutes the boundary between 'awareness of the nature of a crime' may be contentious. But now the amendment stated that 'a person under the age of eighteen at the time of the crime cannot be sentenced to death and must be sentenced to indefinite detention'.

Committee after committee would continue to sit and deliberate in the decades after the Smith case, and it was really only the beginning of reform and radical rethinking of the issues surrounding capital punishment. It is ironic that a tale like this from a small village well off the beaten track should have such repercussions. But it did, and local writers look into the case again from time to time, trying to find out more about the Scawby connection. In the end we probably have to accept that we may never know any more about the family Harold Smith left in order to go and make his contribution to the general funds. But twenty-five years after his outburst and his pulling of the shotgun trigger, his actions were again the subject of discussion when England was moving closer to abolishing the use of the scaffold and noose to deter would-be killers.

There had been a long campaign against capital punishment in the press and in popular literature, and this played a part in the first serious contemplation of the hanging of young people in 1908. A much-reprinted set of verses played a part in this, with the powerful lines,

> The dreadful drop, the hooded head,
> the same for man or woman!
> Were fitter for a nation bred
> In savagery inhuman.

These lines by Alex Gardner appeared in his collection *Law Lyrics* in 1897. They were quoted again in the inter-war years when stories such as Harold Smith's appeared in the tabloids. By 1930 there had been much more attention paid to most aspects of the criminal justice process and indeed to the penal system. Of all the clamours for reform, the one pressing for a close reappraisal of capital punishment was the most public and insistent. The

The hanging site, Cobb Hall. From this tower the condemned would see their last of Lincoln. (Author's Collection)

The condemned prisoner's cell, Lincoln Castle. This bare, small room was where the condemned spent his or her last night. (Author's Collection)

Waddingham today. This picturesque village has remained almost unchanged since the 1930s. (Author's Collection)

Robert Jacklin talking to Superintendent Dalby, in a sketch by Laura Carter, from an early newspaper report.

Harold Smith case would become a touchstone for future social scientists and criminologists with a cause to promote.

In their 1961 landmark study, *Hanged by the Neck*, Arthur Koestler and C.H. Rolph faced the question of hanging young people and this was their conclusion: 'That 50 of the 123 executed in 1949–60, i.e. 41%, were under twenty-five years of age and that of the recommendations to mercy, more than half referred to these. To hang someone under twenty-five every two months, as we were doing then, and to defend this routine on the grounds that they are incapable of reform, amounts to a repudiation of modern penology and of common sense.' These authors were challenging the whole 'doctrine of maximum severity' on which capital punishment had rested for so long. They also asked questions about why the Court of Appeal (established in 1907) had apparently been very limited and narrow in reappraising so many cases where decisions affecting life or death outcomes were handled in a seemingly cursory manner.

It makes an interesting contrast to note that in 1955 at Lincoln Assizes eighteen-year-old David Dennis was found not guilty of capital murder but simply murder, and was sentenced to life imprisonment. There is a striking similarity with the Smith case: Dennis killed his grandparents in their bedroom. The only major difference is that Dennis had taken alcohol; Smith merely felt that he had been shouted at and criticised once too often. He did not need the prompting of strong drink to drive him to the edge of reason.

The Home Secretary, Sir Herbert Samuel (1870–1963). His decision determined Smith's fate. (Laura Carter)

In the same year, 1931, in the south of the county, the village of Gedney, down towards the fens, was the venue for a most extraordinary death: almost certainly a murder of a son by his father, but at the time, and in court, the farmer's dog was a possible suspect. The process of the investigation was to include the services of the famous forensic scientist, Sir Bernard Spilsbury, and this, along with a long period of embarrassment for the local police, makes it a fascinating case.

It all began one morning in December when retired Metropolitan Police officer George Kitchen walked out to the barn on his farm at Gedney with his son, James. George had rented this farm out in the lonely Lincolnshire Fens around Holbeach from the county council. The place was large and he worked it with his two sons, James and William. It was a sharp contrast to his life in London, of course, but the family seemed to be doing fairly well.

On this morning the group carried a loaded shotgun with them. It was the usual practice in that area because there was often the chance of shooting down a goose or a duck for the table. The gun was propped against a shed. They began to prepare for work outside the barn, cleaning their spades with water from a puddle. James's dog, Prince, was with them, a dog described

The scene of the crime, Holme Farm, in a drawing by Laura Carter, taken from an early report.

Gedney, the quintessential south Lincolnshire village, still little changed from the time of this case.
(Laura Carter)

by a neighbour as 'strong and likely to be excited'. On this morning, as they set to work, there was a gunshot and James fell to the ground, mortally wounded. His father, who was seen by two cyclists, ran for help and met a Mr March nearby. The two men went to carry James into the barn. All George said to March was, 'Come on, Jim's shot!' March noticed that George was very upset. But nothing could be done for the young man, and he died after a few minutes. He had been bleeding from his side. The key to the main door of the farmhouse was in his pocket, and the door locked.

When the police arrived George's first statement was that he had carried the gun, and he had leaned it against the meal-house wall 2 feet from the door and with the butt a foot from the wall. The gun was loaded in both barrels and both hammers were up, i.e. cocked. This was so that it was 'ready to shoot any geese'. He said that 'the dog must have knocked the gun down' while his son was cleaning his shovel, at about eight-thirty. He just heard his son say 'Oh' and then fall down.

At the first hearing, in the police court at Holbeach, on 27 January 1932, there was a rare balance of horror and farce. G.R. Paling, prosecuting, said that George had now recalled that he was 'levelling muck' when he became aware that his son had let Prince out of the house. At about eight-twenty a gunshot was heard. Various witnesses said that they had heard the report of the gun, come to the scene, and heard from the father that he had no idea what had caused the gun to go off, apart from the dog.

George Kitchen, in a drawing by Laura Carter, taken from an early report.

The barn, the scene of the shooting. Laura Carter's drawing shows the barn on which the gun was propped.

This was going to be a difficult case for the Chief Constable of the county, Lieutenant Colonel Halland. Here was a man of sixty-three, a retired police officer with two sons, one of whom, 36-year-old James, was now inexplicably dead, and the word spreading around the Fens was that he had been shot by a dog. As the question of whether or not the gun could have been fired if knocked over by the dog needed to be answered, he contacted Sir Bernard Spilsbury.

Before anything else happened in the legal process there had been an inquest at the family home, and it was concluded most likely to be an accident. But as time passed and investigations continued other aspects began to emerge. Tales were told of George chasing his son with a gun on one occasion, and they had quarrelled recently. George was arrested and taken into custody on 12 January. As Sergeant Lown arrested him, Mrs Kitchen said that she would stake her life on his innocence. She then fainted, as her husband was taken to gaol at Spalding.

Then the whole case escalated as Spilsbury got to work, and it was scheduled to be heard at the Old Bailey. It had become an issue that could apparently only be resolved with the testimony of expert witnesses. Spilsbury was a very eminent man; he had been the one most responsible for condemning Dr Crippen in 1910, and he had worked energetically on dozens of high-profile murder cases in the years since. He had now started looking at the ballistics of the incident.

With him in court was the gun expert Robert Churchill. He confirmed that the gun in question was a 12-bore double-barrelled gun of a modern design, and his most important statement was that the pulls were heavy and that it was not possible to jar the gun at full cock. There was no scorch-mark on James's overcoat and Spilsbury was to pay attention to this when working out the trajectory of the cartridge. Spilsbury and Churchill had worked together just eight years before, in the case of the teenage murderer Merrett.

Spilsbury's post mortem showed that the wounds were caused from above, then downwards and forwards. In other words, the likelihood was that the gun had been fired by someone from the hip or shoulder. Another expert, Mr Paling, confirmed that this was the likely account of the firing, suggesting also that, as the wound had fractured two ribs, the shot came from an angle of 55 degrees. His tests indicated that when the gun was fired the muzzle must have been about a yard from the victim. He stressed that 'the gun could only have been discharged by human agency'.

This case had a damaging effect on the reputation of the expert, Robert Churchill. He had a very prestigious position in the world of shooting and gun-making. His shop, close to the National Gallery in Trafalgar Square, had a cellar in which he conducted tests with firearms when he was working for the police. Everyone involved in the criminal law as a professional knew and respected Churchill's work. Churchill had actually visited the Kitchens' farm in December, and he had been sure then that the gun could not have been discharged by the dog knocking it over. He said that 'the pull required to discharge the left barrel was so heavy that I was able to lift the gun at full cock off the ground with my finger hooked round the trigger, without releasing the action. The right trigger needed a traction engine to pull it.' With this kind of certainty, it is amazing to learn that the subsequent events almost wrecked this man's career, and the spin-off story of Churchill and the accusation that he had interfered with the gun (and therefore the evidence) is almost as sensational as the trial itself.

Churchill took the gun to his laboratory in London. Here he found that it would require a mean pressure of 7lb on the trigger to shoot it. This was fully 2lb of pressure heavier than the normal pull. In his typically thorough way, Churchill used tests in which a series of shots were fired at steel and leather from varying distances. He was certain, after all this work, that the wounds that killed young Kitchen could not have been self-inflicted. He also

Engraved for The Malefactor's Register.

The New SESSIONS-HOUSE, *in the Old Bailey*

The Old Bailey. Inside these walls the farcical discussion about the dog, Prince, took place. He was made to stand on a table inside the courtroom. (Author's Collection)

agreed with Spilsbury that the wound could not have been inflicted by a freak accident, such as the weapon being knocked over by the dog. It was after his written report based on these tests was delivered that George Kitchen was arrested in Lincolnshire.

The problems for Churchill began when the defence barristers called in Sir Sydney Smith and a group of other ballistics experts. This phalanx of scientists was so formidable that their testimony led to Churchill being accused of removing the locks of the gun when he first examined it. One of the new experts said that Churchill should have made a test – one in which the cocked and loaded gun would have to be dropped fifty times to see if the accident was possible – rather than rely solely on the scientific and mechanical evidence. On 23 March 1932 poor Churchill was told by a Major

Burrard that a new test was to be made, and it was one that would challenge Churchill's opinion. But before this was done the Lincolnshire officer who arrested Kitchen, Sergeant Lown, made a statement to the effect that the action of the gun had been interfered with (by Churchill) to make it less likely to be fired if it were to be knocked by accident. There were marks on the gun suggesting this, and Churchill's defence was that the marks were there when he first saw it.

From then on Churchill was being tried, as well as George Kitchen. The defence stated in court that Churchill had purposely meddled with the weapon, in order to prove that accidental firing was impossible. Burrard told the Home Secretary that Churchill had filed a part of the gun so that the action of the weapon would conform to the facts given in his evidence. This was a very serious charge. The expert had to give a written reply to the Home Secretary, after Kitchen had been acquitted of course. Churchill said:

> The lock was in this state when I returned it to the Old Bailey and I honestly believe that these witnesses have made a mistake, firstly in examining the lock whilst at full cock, and I should have given evidence to that effect should I have been called. . . . I repeat that if anything had happened to this gun to my knowledge I should have told you. I have given evidence as a gun expert for you for nearly 22 years and never before has expert evidence been called against me.

Churchill was not only rattled, he was indignant and clearly trying to restrain very powerful feelings as he sat down to write this defence of his probity and professionalism. He had a point; to that date all his work in forensic experiment and testimony had been exemplary. Burrard had based his thought on the notion of probability, not analysis of the material quality of the weapon; he had taken one expert's belief in this, who had said that the test of dropping the gun fifty times could easily have been done, and danger eliminated by using sawdust in the cartridges in place of powder. With hindsight, it seems that Burrard's exclamation of shock when he said, 'My God, it has been tampered with' (when five forensic experts were standing with him) was possibly legal histrionics: a piece of drama. But that detail about the marks on the gun was almost to ruin Churchill.

All this scandal continued after the trial itself, which in the end was as inconclusive as the furore among the ballistics experts. Nothing was ever going to show that the father had killed his son. There was no certainty in anything, and the outrageous accusations levelled at Churchill simply diverted attention away from Kitchen, and even from the dog. And what linked the dog with the arguable probability of accidental firing was George Kitchen's first statement that the dog's thick otter tail was perhaps the cause of the firing. But Spilsbury, when asked by the judge if there was any evidence to convict the suspect, said that 'there was nothing exact' to explain how James Kitchen had died.

The whole affair had become, at least in the perception of the newspaper-reading public, a confrontation between 'experts' with the added dark shadow of an accusation of malpractice. First the dog, the 'silent witness' as reporters called him, had stolen the media show limelight, and then the battle of the gunsmiths. The possible murder was almost forgotten in all this.

Reports of George's words and behaviour to his son were given at the trial; a man who let the Kitchens borrow his gun a year earlier testified that there had been what could be described as a feud going on between father and son at that time. He recalled a series of encounters between them and expressed it in this way: 'The accused came in and started shouting. He was rather excited. His son asked him what the — he was shouting about. He talked of his embarrassment in having such a father. I treated the accused to a pint and went to another public house further up the road. We had been there a few moments when the accused came in. He passed a remark and said he was not wanted, all that stuff.' George had apparently then said, and in public, to his son: 'You don't want me. There will be an end to this. I will do you in. I will cripple you.'

Through all this the media had been running a comic and sensational story centred on the dog. Its general tenor was that of 'man shot by own dog'. But then, in court, the dog did become the focus of attention. The 'silent witness' sat in a prominent place in the courtroom. He was brought in and placed on a solicitor's table, where he sat contentedly, wagging his tail. Before the account of the dog was given the other son, William, gave evidence: he said that he had once seen his father chasing his brother with a hatchet, and also with a gun (though it was unloaded). In the face of this, what profit could there be in analysing the nature of the dog? No time was wasted on this but, nevertheless, Mr Justice Swift was tiring of the lack of definite evidence. What happened next was summed up by the *Lincolnshire, Boston and Spalding Free Press*: 'Murder trial stopped. Kitchen discharged. The silent witness (dog) on solicitor's table. Prisoner's remark from the dock. London, Tuesday.'

Sir Bernard Spilsbury had agreed with the judge that in spite of all the evidence assembled and the statements given, there was no clear account of what had actually happened at Brook House Farm that cold December morning. There were all kinds of speculation about what happened, and even suicide was considered, as a cigarette had been found blocking the dead man's trachea. However, it was decided that the sudden shock of being shot had made him swallow.

The summary of what happened leaves many unanswered questions. Basically, a man and his son had gone out to do some farm work and left a loaded and cocked gun leaning against a wall. A dog had then been let out of the house and, as the father's back was turned, a shot had been fired and his son wounded. When the father had run for help, he had been observed to be in a state of distress. The possibilities would have charmed Conan Doyle:

(a) The dog may have knocked the gun over, but ballistics experts insisted this would not have been possible.
(b) The forensic evidence points directly to the only other known person on the scene, George Kitchen. But what was his motive?
(c) If there was another person, where was the evidence of his presence and, again, what would be his motive?

The farm buildings were locked and secure. If there had been a robber, and he had been in there for some time, why would he need to kill anyway? He would have simply made a quiet escape while the two men were working.

Even if there had been a solid case against the father, it seems very unlikely that this was a premeditated murder. The general mystification and bafflement in the area had been made worse from the very beginning by the reconstruction the local police had staged at the barn. By torchlight they tried to ascertain if it was possible for the gun to have been triggered by the actions of the dog. Farcically there was a crowd of people watching. Obviously, general talk about the affair went in the direction of making fun of the whole business of the dog's involvement. In court, the attention paid to the dog was such that some thought a little tab on the collar could have caught the trigger, and there was a demonstration of the tying of Prince's collar. At the beginning of the case, before the father's arrest, parents kept their children at home for some days, concluding there was a homicidal maniac loose in the Fens.

The whole local culture and lifestyle included guns and dogs, and always had done. Kitchen himself was a strong, sturdy man, had been a London copper and knew how to handle guns. He was clearly familiar with violence. But in the end even the experts' opinion differed. Spilsbury thought the gun had been fired from 3 feet; Paling thought much closer. It had to be said, though, that there was nothing conclusive in the experts' theories.

George Kitchen made a statement after the Old Bailey trial, saying that he 'needed a rest'. He pointed out that he had no idea what he was going to do in the future. The whole family status and enterprise was finished and there would always be a stain of suspicion on him. He soon left the area and was not heard of again. There is no record of where he went.

For the charismatic Bernard Spilsbury, a major celebrity trapped in a bizarre regional mystery, this was arguably the strangest case in his hundreds of investigations. He conducted 25,000 post mortems, and it was a brave man who would dare to challenge his opinions in court. But he had to accept the Gedney death as 'untidy' by his rigorous scientific standards. His reputation, however, was certainly not tarnished in any way by his foray into Lincolnshire. He was known to win by force of character backed by sheer factual and analytical skill. But the question of the dog killing his master defied even his notable abilities.

In the same year, then, Lincolnshire had experienced two killings in places well away from the major towns; in both cases there had been family members shot, and in ordinary daily situations. Both cases had hit the headlines but for very different reasons. In Waddingham the incident was destined to force an examination of capital punishment; in Gedney it tested forensic science to the limits. Even with hindsight and the more sophisticated forensics at our disposal today, it is still hard to imagine the Gedney case being solved. The only logical conclusion is that Kitchen's rages led him to the real thing: firing a shot at his son. But there is no evidence at all that this was so. Logical conclusions do not always agree with legal ones.

10

MURDER IN THE FAMILY

Kirkby-on-Bain, 1934

There are dozens of reasons for calling this case the most significant and contentious in the history of crime in Lincolnshire. Reappraisals of the reasons why Ethel Major was hanged in Hull prison for the murder of her husband a few days before Christmas 1934 have been made regularly over the years. The problem is that nothing can turn the clock back, and re-examining this case is a painful business.

The outline of the case is reasonably straightforward, but a controversy will follow. The Majors, lorry driver Arthur and wife Ethel, lived in Kirkby-on-Bain near Horncastle with their fifteen-year-old son. They were not happily married; she was forty-two and her husband forty-four. Arthur had a drink problem and was very difficult to live with. He also appeared to be having an affair with a neighbour, a Mrs Kettleborough, and Ethel said that she had seen two love letters written by this woman to her husband. Hard though it is to believe in hindsight, Ethel Major showed these to her family doctor and said these words to him: 'A man like that is not fit to live, and I will do him in.'

Arthur Major died as a result of what was defined as an epileptic fit, but then, before the funeral could take place, this anonymous letter arrived on the desk of Inspector Dodson of Horncastle police:

Sir, have you ever heard of a wife poisoning her husband? Look further into the death (by heart failure) of Mr Major of Kirkby-on-Bain. Why did he complain of his food

A sketch of Ethel Major by Laura Carter from a contemporary photograph.

Kirkby-on-Bain was another small community which was rather isolated in Ethel Major's time.
(Laura Carter)

tasting nasty and throw it to a neighbour's dog, which has since died? Ask the undertaker if he looked natural after death? Why did he stiffen so quickly? Why was he so jerky when dying? I myself have heard her threaten to poison him years ago. In the name of the law, I beg you to analyse the contents of his stomach.

This was signed 'Fairplay'. A coroner's order stopped the interment and Major's body was examined again. The coffin was actually removed in the presence of the mourners. Ethel was in her house with relatives, including Arthur's two brothers, when the police arrived. 'It looks as though they're suspicioning me', she told her father, and he agreed. Ethel, small, fragile and short-sighted, was an unassuming woman with some quirky habits and a complicated nature.

It soon emerged that the dog, a wire-haired terrier, had indeed died after having muscular spasms. The pathologist, Dr Roche Lynch of St Mary's

Hospital, Paddington, also confirmed that Arthur Major's body had in it a quantity of strychnine sufficient to kill him. The surface of his body was blue, and almost any contact on the skin initiated a spasm. The average fatal dose for a man was between one and two grains, and Arthur had 1.27 and the dog 0.12. Lynch opined that Major had taken two doses, one on 22 May 1934 and the fatal one on 24 May. To dismiss any possibility of suicide, Lynch said, 'On account of the awful agony he would go through, I do not think that any would-be suicide would take it a second time, unless he were insane.'

It had been a terrible and agonising death. His son Lawrence saw Arthur walk into the front room with his head between his hands. He went out and Lawrence saw him fall over. He was put to bed. Ethel's father, Tom Brown, came later and saw Arthur foaming at the mouth and in the throes of violent spasms. When Dr Smith came later, he made up his mind that this was epilepsy. It took a long time for the man to die. In court it was revealed that Ethel had left him alone all night, and in the morning had gone shopping. Later in the day he seemed to recover and he actually drank some tea, but then there was a relapse. Virtually the last words Arthur Major spoke to his wife were, 'You have been good to me.'

Ethel Major was interviewed by Chief Inspector Hugh Young of Scotland Yard, and he gave an account of her in which she stated that her husband had died of eating some corned beef. 'She appeared over-eager to impress me with the fact that she had nothing to do with providing his meals, explaining that for a fortnight before her husband's death she and her son had stayed with her father . . .' Young was eager to point out that Ethel was a cool and resourceful woman and that she 'showed no pangs of sorrow at the loss of her husband'.

The crucially important statement made by Ethel to Young was, 'I did not know my husband had died from strychnine poisoning,' and Young replied, 'I never mentioned strychnine poisoning. How did you know that?' As H. Montgomery Hyde pointed out in his biography of Lord Birkett, in Birkett's time poisoning 'was considered such a repulsive crime that convicted prisoners were practically never reprieved'.

When Ethel Major was arrested and charged the full story emerged and Lord Birkett, talented as he was, knew that he would lose this case. There was too much evidence against her. At Lincoln Assizes on 30 October 1934 she appeared before Mr Justice Charles. Richard O'Sullivan and P.E. Sandlands prosecuted, and Ethel pleaded not guilty.

One of the most convincing pieces of evidence against her was the fact that she had a key belonging to a chest in which her father, Tom Brown, used to store strychnine; this was used to kill vermin. Tom Brown testified he had lost the key some years before and had had a new one made. When Sandlands brought out a key, Brown confirmed it was the one he had lost. It had been in

Ethel Major's possession. There was also a hexagonal green bottle for storing strychnine in the chest; this had been found in the Majors' house. Then came further information that Ethel had had access to her father's house. She had known where a key was hidden outside, and a purse she had containing the chest key was confirmed as being one that belonged to her mother.

Tom Brown was questioned about this key. Here is a point of real fascination: the father was testifying against his daughter. Lord Birkett must have seen this as another nail in the coffin for his already flimsy defence. There Brown was in the witness-box: a whiskered old countryman. Regarding the key, the prosecution pointed out that it had turned up in Ethel Major's possession 'shining as though it had been recently polished'. Birkett desperately tried to retrieve the situation by saying that lots of women carried trivial objects and mementos around in their handbags. In other words, she may have had the purse and key, but not the strychnine. Tom Brown had looked at the little bottle and suggested that it seemed to have the same amount in it as it had had the last time he looked at it.

The heart of the situation was the strychnine and the corned beef she knew was her husband's last meal. Ethel had admitted that she knew some corned beef in the cupboard was not really edible and yet she had left it, saying nothing to anyone. She had known Arthur was due to eat it. Looking into the tale of the corned beef was to be important in court. Contradictory things were said about the purchase of the tin of beef, Ethel saying Arthur had sent Lawrence to buy it, and Lawrence saying the opposite. All this cast doubt on Ethel's statement, though it has to be said that the retailer recalled that Lawrence had come for the beef and said that his father had given him the money to buy it.

Tom Brown did, however, have quite a lot to say about Arthur Major's character, relating that when Brown's first wife had died in 1929 Arthur had come to the Browns' place very drunk and had used threatening words. Ethel Major's natural daughter, Auriel Brown, was asked about the love letters and the supposed affair Arthur was having with Mrs Kettleborough. Birkett knew that if there was any chink in the armour of the prosecution's case it was the possibility of provocation with regard to this affair. The focus of their dialogue was not promising in this respect.

Mr Birkett: 'Did you ever see anything that you thought suspicious between Mrs Kettleborough and Major?'

Auriel: 'I saw them once making eyes at each other. Mrs Kettleborough was always outside the house when Major came home. She put herself in his way.'

Mr Birkett: 'The advances that you saw were on one side?'

Auriel: 'Both sides.'

A great deal more information about the Majors' life together was to emerge. They hated the very sight of each other; Arthur Major had severe financial problems and was of the opinion that his wife was a spendthrift and was helping to ruin him. Only a few days before he died he had placed an announcement in the local paper, the *Horncastle News*, declaring himself not responsible for any debts his wife had accrued. The situation at the Majors' was far worse than many around the village would ever have suspected.

One fundamental cause of their rift was the fact that Ethel, before she met Arthur, had given birth to a child (Auriel) in 1914, when she was only twenty-three. She never revealed the name of the father, and the girl was brought up as a daughter of the Browns. This refusal to give details of the business infuriated Arthur; things deteriorated so much that she left him for a while, returning to her family home.

In court at Lincoln, Lord Birkett later wrote, he knew the verdict of the jury when they came back into court after an hour's deliberation because none of them looked in Ethel's direction. They found her guilty, but with a recommendation for mercy. Ethel collapsed and moaned that she was innocent as she was carried away.

There was a strong feeling that a formal appeal was a waste of time, but Birkett did join a group of lawyers who petitioned the Home Secretary for a reprieve. The response was that there were 'insufficient grounds to justify him in advising His Majesty to interfere with the due course of law'. One last ditch appeal came from the Lord Mayor of Hull, in the form of a telegram to the King and Queen, pleading for their intervention.

On 19 December Ethel Major was executed by Thomas Pierrepoint, with the Under Sheriff of Lincolnshire present. As usual, the Governor, Captain Roberts, made the statement about the hanging being done in 'a humane and expeditious manner'.

In many ways this was only the beginning of the Ethel Major story. After all, the sentence was based on circumstantial evidence and there were certainly factors of provocation, an argument that she was not her normal self when she acted, and that there was considerable enmity and aggression towards her from her husband.

A closer and more searching account of Ethel Major's life is helpful in understanding these events, and why there have been so many reassessments of the case. She was born Ethel Brown in Monkton Bottom, Lincolnshire, in 1891. Her father was a gamekeeper and they lived on the estate of Sir Henry Hawley. By all accounts, as a child she lived a good life with her parents and her three brothers, going to a small school at Coningby and then at Mareham le Fen. She stayed at home for some years, learning dressmaking and the usual domestic skills. Then came the liaison with the unknown lover and her pregnancy. Some writers make something of this with regard to her later criminality, pointing out that five out of eight women hanged in Britain in prominent cases had illegitimate children. There is no significance in this, it simply illustrates the need some writers on crime have to find patterns and profiles.

Ethel had known Arthur Major when they were children. In 1907 he left the area to live in Manchester, but then, in the First World War, he joined the Manchester Regiment and they began to meet. When he was wounded and hospitalised back home, in Bradford, they wrote to each other. Keeping the truth about Auriel quiet until they were married was perhaps the basic error in her understanding of her new husband's personality. In court, in 1934, there was to be a great deal said about potential provocation on the part of Arthur Major, and even more written in years to come.

Birkett cross-examined Lawrence in an attempt to provide a clearer picture of Arthur Major's character traits. Lawrence confirmed that his father came home drunk almost every night and that this had become more severe in recent months. The topic then shifted to violence and fear.

Birkett: 'When he was in that state, did he quarrel violently with your mother?'

Lawrence: 'Yes, if we were in.'

When Ethel and her son retreated to Tom Brown's, they would sleep on a couch in the kitchen or in a garden shed, Lawrence sleeping in his top-coat and all his day-clothes. A story of provocation and mitigating circumstances began to emerge. In 1931 Ethel Major had taken out a summons for separation, so violent had his behaviour been, but Arthur made vows to reform his life and Ethel changed her mind. Tom Brown had confirmed, 'Major used violent and filthy language to his wife and also threatened her.'

As in most marital situations of such conflict, questions are asked about the nature of the relationship and whether or not there really is a victim and an aggressor. At this trial Judge Charles and indeed Norman Birkett used this approach. Birkett boldly asked young Lawrence, 'Should I be right in saying that your mother all your life has been very kind to you, and your father very wicked?' Judge Charles went ahead and asked witnesses in general about where blame might lie.

Therefore we have such questions as, 'What sort of a fellow was Major?' and 'Did you ever see him the worse for liquor?' One could guess the outcome of this. Such people as the vicar's wife and the rector talked of Major as 'sober' as far as they knew. He was a man with a very amiable public persona, yet inside his own home he was often monstrous to his own family.

If we turn to the other element in potential defence of provocation, the subject of the love letters comes up. What exactly was the truth about Arthur Major and his affair? We need to recall here that Major was very active in the village, not only doing voluntary work for the church, but putting in time as a local councillor. Ethel's report was that she found some love letters in their bedroom, and of course this has the implication that she had been searching for evidence after so much innuendo and whispering about an 'affair'. One such letter was this, which was read out in court:

To my dearest sweetheart,
In answer to your dear letter received this morning, thank you dearest.
The Postman was late I was waiting a long time for him . . . I see her
watching you In the garden . . . Well, sweetheart, I will close with
fondest love to my Precious one . . .

From your loving sweetheart,
Rose

When she faced Arthur with her new knowledge (she had already told her
doctor, Dr Armour), he said he would do nothing. The issue became a cause
and a local crusade for Ethel; she wrote complaints about her husband to
the local police and even tried to change the terms of the leasehold of their
property so that she could be classed as a 'tenant'. The natural end of this was
a talk with a solicitor, and a letter was drafted, as she said, on behalf of her
husband, warning Mrs Rose Kettleborough not to write again. This solicitor
had witnessed Major making violent threats against Ethel, but not taken it to
be anything serious.

The Kettleboroughs in court provide a record of what can only be called
tittle-tattle, and some of the discussion of the case on record seems entirely
trivial; yet when Rose herself took the stand there was clearly something
interesting to come. This fur-coat clad, small, attractive woman said that she
had never 'been out' with Arthur Major. She also denied loitering to wait for
Arthur by the house, as Auriel had said.

When the subject of the letters came up, Birkett tried very hard to do some
amateur handwriting analysis, comparing the orthography and style in the
love letters to other writing she had done. Nothing was achieved by this,
and even an exploration of her past knowledge of Arthur led to nothing
significant. To sum up, Birkett attempted every ploy he could think of but in
the end the record of the trial can be made to read more like an indulgence in
small-scale scandal than a murder case.

But this is not the end of the saga of Ethel Major. A study of the case by
Annette Ballinger in her book *Dead Women Walking* (2000) takes a closer
look at the provocation line of thought. She pays attention to comments made
at the time about the discontent in the Major home, such as the statement by a
solicitor's clerk that 'Arthur often threatened his wife. I gather that their home
life was unhappy.' She also puts great emphasis on the change in Major as he
drank more. His son's words, 'The drink was having an effect on my father, he
was not the man he had been', do imply an almost submerged narrative that
has only been re-examined many years after Ethel's death.

For Ballinger, it was the issue of the right to remain silent that shaped
Ethel's destiny. The factors that stood out most prominently in court – the
fact that the day before Major's death he had withdrawn from responsibility
for her debts, and her husband's apparent condition of being a poor victim

Hull Prison in a drawing by Andy Tennick. (Author's Collection)

– made her silence worse. As Ballinger notes, 'the case of Ethel Major demonstrates how the prisoner's right to remain silent could be interpreted as evidence of guilt. Thus the judge referred to Ethel's non-appearance in the witness box no less than six times in his summing up.'

The 1898 Criminal Evidence Act had made the 'right to silence' concept very important in the construction of defences, but the unfortunate, unforeseen side effect of this was that juries tended to interpret silence as guilt in many cases. This interpretation ignored the fact that some people in the dock were nervous, apprehensive or even, in some cases, had been advised by their brief to say nothing.

Ballinger sees Ethel Major as a 'battered woman' and notes that generally such women are too traumatised to give evidence. One common view of the time, and this is something that helps us understand her situation, was, according to Linda Gordon, that beating was 'part of a general picture of slovenly behaviour, associated with drunkenness, and squalor of the wife's own making'.

Finally, if the notion of Ethel's failure to safeguard her reputation is on the agenda in this notorious case, then aspects of her behaviour in the village have to be an important factor in understanding how she was perceived and judged in court. Her eccentric questioning of various neighbours, her interviews with the doctor and her letters to the press all add up to give a picture of a woman who was both desperate and indeed in a very nervous state. Her documented behaviour, as she worked hard to put things right in the household, only made her situation worse. Of course in court these actions would reinforce the moral condemnation of her as someone who had had a bastard child earlier in her life and not told her husband about it.

She was judged for being generally bad tempered, and this was made more prominent than her husband's equally capricious and aggressive behaviour. On one occasion she had thrown a brick and had 'embarked on a wild round of revenge and malice that included half the population of the village', according to another commentary on the case.

The executioner at the time, Albert Pierrepoint, wrote about the other way women killers need to be seen: not as the hard, rational poisoners of the media images, but as 'ordinary women, rarely beautiful . . . Square faced, thin mouthed, eyes blinking behind National Health glasses . . . hair scraped thin by curlers, lumpy ankles above homely shoes . . .' As Annette Ballinger has said, 'poison was responsible for her death'. When Ethel Major's case started covering the main pages of newspapers the whole back-list of women poisoners was invoked. All the images of women using arsenic on husbands, from Mary Ann Cotton back in the mid-Victorian period, to the earlier Lincolnshire instances, were on the stage as the sad story unfolded. For decades the pages of the *Police Gazette* had been full of lurid tales of women poisoners; what hope was there for truth to emerge when the media had categorised them as the worst kind of heartless killers?

Alderman Stark of Hull, when he wrote a last appeal for clemency, saying, 'For the sake of humanity I implore you to reconsider your decision, especially having regard to the nearness of Christmas . . . The heartfelt pleas contained in this telegram are those of 300,000 inhabitants and particularly those of the women of this great city', was fighting more than a judicial decision. He was going against the grain of many centuries of myths built around the 'female of the species is more deadly than the male' notion.

The sense of defeat and the inevitable conclusion on the scaffold was hovering over her defence from the beginning. Lord Birkett's memoirs contain his view that Crown Counsel had opened with a statement that had a ring of finality: '. . . the case is really on the evidence unanswerable'. One of the very best defence lawyers in the land could do nothing. With this in mind, it seems odd that the *Daily Express* had insisted that 'nobody believes she will be hanged' just a few weeks before the sentence.

There was no way that an appeal based on the unfairness of the judge's summing up would succeed. Whoever 'Fairplay' was who sent the anonymous letter, he or she had opened the path to the gallows for Ethel Major, and the only consolation, looking back over the years, is that the Pierrepoints were very skilled men in their trade. Ethel would have left this world very speedily indeed, though they must have felt something similar to John Ellis's reactions when he hanged Edith Thompson in 1922: 'My own feelings defy description. . . . I kept telling myself that the only humane course was to work swiftly and cut her agony as short as possible.' This is a stark reminder of the feelings of James Berry when he dealt with Mary Lefley.

Unfortunately, in spite of all the above discussion of this fascinating case study, the reference books will always contain the same kind of simplified statements as these words from Gaute and O'Dell's *The Murderers' Who's Who* (1979): 'Major, Ethel Lillie. A 43-year-old Lincolnshire gamekeeper's daughter who murdered her husband with strychnine.' The woman who never gave evidence at her trial is being judged by posterity, and is still enveloped in silence. In modern terms, and with a more feminist, open-minded view of *mens rea*, the mind-set to take a life, it can be argued that in 1934 there was a too narrow definition of intention, because the accused is supposed to see the same probability that the jury see, in the way that the intention is given to them by lawyers interpreting the defendant's actions.

But all that would have been far too subtle for the court in Ethel Major's case.

11
ATTACK IN THE KITCHEN

Scunthorpe, 1945

Scunthorpe has always been about iron and steel, and although today the visitor who drives in from the west from Doncaster has to look hard to see the towering blast furnaces, from the Brigg Road, the massive steelworks is still a dominating presence over the town. In years gone by, before the steel industry contracted and the Normanby Park site was closed, the industry was kept going by thousands of workers living in the Crosby and Brumby areas of the town.

Ravendale Street, where the house was. An army services canteen was here in 1945. (Author's Collection)

Even today, when so much has changed, the centre of Scunthorpe has housing in long terraces of red brick, with gaps between called 'ten-foots' locally. In the early and mid-twentieth century, large numbers of people lived close together in these warrens of side streets and back alleys. They were not only the scene of close family ties but also of some nasty crimes, and many townsfolk were vulnerable: old people, women alone at night and anyone seen to be weak and an easy target for robbery were open to assault, and as with every other town with casual labour and a transient element in the population, trouble in the streets was not uncommon.

In the 1950s, for instance, people living in those streets made sure that doors were locked and back gates made secure. Such a careful person was 69-year-old Emily Charlesworth, who lived at 4 Ravendale Street and worked as a live-in housekeeper for steelworker Harry Ramshaw, and had been in that capacity for many years. Emily was born in Scunthorpe, was an active church worker and, as the *Evening Telegraph* reported at the time, was 'known in the neighbourhood as a quiet, unassuming woman' who had 'worked for some years as nursemaid to a clergyman's family in Australia'. She had come home to Scunthorpe twenty-seven years before, in 1918. But on 23 September 1945 all her care about security came to nothing and she was found battered to death in her kitchen.

Ramshaw found her body when he returned from the night-shift at 6 a.m. He had left his home at 9.30 the previous evening to be on time for the ten o'clock shift. He found her in the kitchen, with the gas light still on. The police initially reported that there had been no signs of a struggle but, when a blood-stained breadknife was found later, it seemed likely that Emily had tried to defend herself. Ramshaw thought no money had been stolen.

The death was the result of extreme violence, yet the motive was not obvious, and this made it a puzzling case from the very beginning. Unusually, too, the back door of the house was unlocked, and there were pots on the table as if she had been entertaining a guest, although she had not changed her clothes for the visit and still wore her working attire.

Ravendale Street at that time was surrounded by other dwellings, which were bordered by an optician and a services canteen. The kitchen faced on to the back yard and the ten-foot, the latter still existing today, though Ramshaw's house is now part of a shop. Bricked-in windows that were part of No. 4 may still be seen. An important detail is that the sitting room was visible from the main thoroughfare of Ravendale Street.

A post mortem was carried out by Dr J.M. Webster of the Home Office, but the result was not available at the inquest on 24 September, so at that stage witnesses were called. A sense of high drama unfolded across the town as people read that top Scotland Yard officers were in town. Chief Inspector Davis and Sergeant Wolf were present, alongside Scunthorpe man Super-intendent Knowler. The coroner then gave more details, describing the state

The back yard. This is now heavily protected, as it should have been at the time. (Author's Collection)

of Emily Charlesworth when found with her head severely battered. Her face was so badly damaged that Ramshaw only recognised her by means of her green jumper and the shape of her figure. Her niece, Edna Warner, was also present at the inquest.

Harry Ramshaw recounted his last words to Emily as he left for work; she had said it was time for him to catch his bus and then, 'Do be careful, Harry.' This last was a reference to the risks involved in his work.

Clearly, attention turned to whether or not there might have been a visitor to Emily that evening. Her niece and Harry both said that this was unlikely. Edna Warner made a point of saying how happy and cheerful her aunt had been when she had last seen her about a month earlier. Even this early in the investigation, there were difficulties, and all the police could say was that they were following a line of enquiry. The pathologist's report was desperately needed.

Meanwhile, a fingerprint expert, Chief Inspector Birch, and a crime scene photographer, Detective Inspector Law, also came north from the Yard.

The whole enquiry was escalating. Local reports were fragmented at this early stage, and the newspapers were eager to snap up any little detail. Some said that a neighbour had heard a scream; another that a vital clue had been found but was not sure what that was. The coroner, Mr Dyson, was told by Knowler that it would be some weeks before the police would be in a position to pass on any important information. The Scunthorpe public had just one image of the poor woman who had died so violently: a photograph taken of her outside the Ravendale Street house when she was much younger. The girl in the photograph is thin and spare, with long arms, short hair and a warm, playful expression on her face. She wears a sleeveless summer dress. No doubt this was Emily back in 1918.

Meanwhile, there was a significant development on 26 September. Because there were no real forensic details, a vagueness about the murder still predominates in the reports, but two details were released: first, a beer bottle had been found in the house, and then accounts of a courting couple being in the ten-foot near the house were given. The local report was speculation, raising the dramatic level of the events: 'A further clue – a stout bottle found on the scene of the crime has been revealed today. The police are making an urgent appeal to customers of a local hotel to inform them of any instance of a person seen taking away a Guinness bottle on Saturday night. The bottle may have an important bearing on the case.'

The report also supposed that Emily was 'unconscious when the fatal blows were struck'. The speculation must have brought about appeals to four local pubs, all within a few hundred yards of the Ravendale Street house. The closest one was on the next block along from Ravendale Street. But of course there was also the neighbouring services canteen, and police thinking linked the man in the courting couple to the army. Apparently there was a sighting and that does seem likely in light of the wider context: men were being demobbed steadily after the end of the war. The servicemen were coming home, many to no work and some to a rootless existence; logically, the police would be thinking of the likelihood of a demobbed man being involved, because Emily's home was so close to a place where they gathered. The ten-foot passageways in the town were then and are still places where lovers meet and youngsters gather. The ten-foot by the murder house is sprayed with graffiti today.

The police were at pains to scale down the level of fear and panic in the town. People were assured that there was no 'homicidal maniac' on the loose and that there had been no previous attacks on women in the area. However, as with most murder cases, all kinds of wild stories surfaced in the gaps between solid information and developments in the investigation. One of the strangest in Scunthorpe was the arrival of a note at the police station from a local medium. This led to the headline, 'Was Murderer Drowned?' The medium claimed she had been 'talking' to the killer, and that he was a

The ten-foot – still a lovers' lane.
(Author's Collection)

serviceman expecting release. He had been to the old lady's home and she had made him tea. The killer claimed he had run away 'in a terrific wind' after the killing, and went on, 'I don't know where I went, but eventually I came to a pond, or water in a dyke. I may have been near the Trent. I just jumped into it. Make it known if you can to those who have it in hand. I was fully dressed so cannot be far away. I would rather not give you my name.' With quiet irony, the reporter noted that 'The police have interviewed the spiritualist.'

Meanwhile, Emily Charlesworth's body was laid to rest at St John's Church in the town, a church she had attended all her life except when abroad. There was a huge crowd outside, and a hush descended on it when the coffin was carried out after the Revd Mr Swaby had completed his sermon and said kind words about the woman. The *Evening Telegraph* noted that the Scotland Yard men were present, and said, 'There was a crowd at the gates of Brumby cemetery when the cortège arrived. At the western end a number of women, some of them with young children standing in front of them, had already lined up near the open grave and only the arrival of the funeral party . . . induced them to move back.' In short, the case was the talk of the town, and there was a sense of outrage. People were saying goodbye to a woman who 'did a lot of small jobs in a very thorough way', as Revd Swaby had said. A woman who sold tickets for church events, kept a clean house and cared for her employer was noteworthy for being ordinary, and so the sense of disgust and revulsion grew, and was to play a part in the next stage of the investigation.

Meanwhile, the search went on for clues or materials in the area. Every house in Scunthorpe and the nearby villages was subject to enquiry and questioning about possible witnesses or sightings of the army man. Five hundred people were interviewed, and the appeal for the courting couple to come forward was sustained. A cryptic announcement was placed in the press about this lead: 'The police believe it is possible that one or other of the couple may have personal reasons for not wishing to reveal their presence in the ten-foot in those circumstances. In that case the companion may come forward and may do so without hesitation. Information from only one of the couple would satisfy the police.'

There was now some kind of profile of the soldier wanted for questioning, and the police communicated that the man was in Oswald Road on the night of the murder and had been seen again in the town since. Oswald Road is only half a mile from the Ramshaw home. He was aged between twenty-five and thirty, about 5 feet 9 inches tall with a pale complexion and large eyes. He had

Scunthorpe Police Court. (Author's Collection)

Emily Charlesworth. (Laura Carter)

been seen wearing a khaki raincoat and carrying a valise. This description practically guaranteed that he was leaving, and if he was he would most probably have been seen, but nothing came of it. When October arrived and there was still no real progress the Scotland Yard men tried to allay people's fears and announced that rumour-mongering and 'hysteria' would not help. But by 2 October the courting couple had been found. The definite clues from the kitchen where the body was found now being considered, the blood-stained breadknife, the Guinness bottle and the blood found on a pair of fire-irons receded into the background. It was only when attention given to the lovers was forgotten and the sensational news that Harry Ramshaw had been charged with the murder that these earlier material details of the crime scene came back into the foreground.

Two of the detectives, Kirby and Davis, had interviewed Ramshaw at Scunthorpe police station, and he had been charged. Ramshaw, unsteady and agitated, came into the magistrates' court to face the charge in a smart blue suit, and only said, 'I have told Inspector Davis all I know.' The full wording of the charge must have been forbidding for this simple, hard-working man: 'On the 22nd of September, in the parish of Scunthorpe, feloniously, wilfully and of his malice aforethought did kill and murder Emily Jane Charlesworth, against the peace of our sovereign lord the King, his crown and dignity.' Ramshaw was shocked; he had made no arrangements for legal aid and wept as he asked for advice. He was given representation and then led away by two officers.

At another police court appearance a few weeks later a fuller picture of the affair was to emerge. First, at last the pathologist's report was now summarised; the attack had been brutal in the extreme. Not a single bone in Emily's face was unbroken. Dr Webster was sure that Emily had fought against her attacker, and that she had also been strangled. On the other hand, the first of many details about Ramshaw began to emerge that were to cast doubt on the whole process of his interrogation and arrest. A Dr Collins had inspected Ramshaw and found that there were no signs of any injury on him: no abrasions or cuts.

Before the magistrates chaired by John Tomlinson, the story was given of what Ramshaw had done that awful night. A neighbour had seen him come out on to the street at 6 a.m. on the Sunday morning; he was crying and saying that his housekeeper was dead. Mr Claxton, for the prosecution, said that the neighbour, Mr Dennis, 'could not get much sense out of him, as he was obviously upset'. Ramshaw then went to the home of another niece, Miss Thompson, in Ethel Street, which was on the end of Cole Street, just a few hundred yards from Ravendale Street. The niece came, then phoned the police. Emily was lying on her back with her arms and legs outstretched.

After 7 a.m., Sergeant Ogilvie arrived and and he also saw that Ramshaw was terribly upset. The scene in the kitchen was a bloodbath. One of the woman's shoes was stuck in blood by the fireplace and blood was splashed on the wall. There was also blood on her stocking-knees. All Ramshaw said was that he spoke to her when he came in from his night shift, and she did not answer. The mess in the room was horrendous; the woman's dentures were on the floor, and her glasses were jammed in her hair, with one lens covered in blood by the side of her head. A bent brass poker lay under the table. Both a sharp and a blunt instrument had been used on her broken face. The bruises on her hands made it clear she had tried to fend off blows coming at her face; she had died by strangulation.

Emily Charlesworth's last day alive had been normal; after doing most of her housework, she had been visited by a Miss Naughton, and they had had a chat in the living room until the visitor left at about a quarter past four. Emily was standing at her front door at six-thirty that evening, and was seen there by a Mrs Cooper. Her friends, giving statements, described the way in which Emily always took precautions to keep the property secure; her habit was to lock the back gate by the ten-foot, the back door, and even put a brick under the gate. 'She was not fond of strangers,' one woman said.

On 27 September CI Davis had started his series of interviews with Ramshaw, and had made the man take him to the murder scene and go through his movements and responses on the morning when he found the body. On 2 October he was interviewed again. At that point he was charged with the murder. He had been under considerable pressure and had asked to go home but was detained.

In court, Ernest Dennis, an engine driver, confirmed that he saw Ramshaw in tears as he came home from work that morning: 'He was crying, shaking all over and was very agitated.' He told Dennis that his housekeeper was dead and that he did not know what to do. He asked Dennis for help. He was sure she was dead because there was blood all over her face. Another neighbour was also a valuable witness: Ellen Foulston, who lived at No. 8 in the street. She awoke at just before six and saw and heard Ramshaw and Dennis outside; she heard Ramshaw say, 'Something terrible has happened to my housekeeper.' She went outside and spoke to them, offering to help. The doctor came and all four people went inside. Again, Foulston confirmed that Ramshaw was 'sobbing'. Ravendale Street is not long; then, the houses were huddled close together and all street noises would easily have been heard. Living two houses away, though, Foulston would not have heard noises from inside No. 4. When asked in court, she said she had heard nothing unusual.

What was the relationship between Ramshaw and Emily? This was becoming an increasingly important question now that Ramshaw was in the spotlight and charged. Miss Thompson was asked for her opinion and said, 'Ramshaw and Miss Charlesworth were very fond of each other.' They lived a routine life, like a couple, and were both very supportive of one another and cooperative. Ramshaw was an industrious man, doing hard physical work. Emily had an established routine and a busy life with church work and housekeeping, with a few close friends.

Dr Collins's evidence about his examination of Ramshaw was to prove crucially important. When he did the examination, four days after the killing, he found nothing to connect him with the attack: 'On his chest, arms, forearms, legs, head, face and hands there were no signs of injury, abrasions or bruises.' He agreed with the pathology report that there had been a desperate struggle for life against the murderer, and that logically marks on the body of the attacker would be expected. His first statement about the time of the attack was to prove important; he said it occurred at around ten hours before his examination, which would place the time of the murder at about eight in the evening of the Saturday.

From 23 October, when Ramshaw's defence counsel began their work, some murky waters were stirred in court, and the Scotland Yard men were in focus. T.J. Lewis, for Ramshaw, probed into the words and attitudes that were generally applied when Ramshaw was questioned. He brought up the mention of 'the noose' waiting for the suspect, and some allegation of torment involving the words, 'I have a good mind to strangle you.' Basically, Ramshaw had said that when he came home on the Sunday morning he had found the gate and back door open. The back-door key had been in the inside of the lock. At that point Ramshaw started to crack in court. He was an emotional wreck, and when a relative of Emily's, her nephew, took the stand, another side of his character began to appear.

This relative was Mr McGlone, and he spoke of Ramshaw's mental state and learning difficulties: 'Why, Harry, you remember what happened before auntie's death. You want to be a man and not have the mind of a child.' This makes the Yard men's story of their interrogation of Ramshaw very questionable. Davis drove Ramshaw to the house, then in the car they had a conversation which suggests that Ramshaw was under extreme pressure and becoming confused and apprehensive. He shook hands with the detective, said 'I wish all this could be over', and was then told that after a night's rest he would be questioned again. Ramshaw allegedly then said, 'I cannot remember touching her . . . I do not want to go down the line of getting a life sentence for it . . . I cannot remember what I have done . . .' Defence stepped in swiftly and insisted that these were not the voluntary words used by the accused man. This was to lead to some very serious allegations against the Yard officers.

Other details that were part of the case against Ramshaw disappeared: the Guinness bottle, for instance; the prosecution had found it very strange that no fingerprints at all of Ramshaw were found in the room. But then, referring to the prints, CI Davis was questioned by Lewis for the defence:

Lewis: 'Are you suggesting that in telling the court of that last suspicion of yours that the accused had removed all traces of fingerprints from every and any article in the room after the crime?'

Davis: 'I make no suggestion.'

Lewis: 'Is not that the logical conclusion? Some persons might infer that.'

The course of the trial was turning in Ramshaw's favour, and such facts as the landlord of the Oswald Hotel saying that he had never seen Ramshaw in the pub at any time, and that there were no prints matching Ramshaw's on the bottle, increased doubts about the guilt of the accused.

The focus then shifted to the mental state of Ramshaw, as hinted at by the nephew of Emily Charlesworth. Lewis fastened on to this, and faced the

Ramshaw (centre) with his family. (Laura Carter)

detective with the delicate question of how Ramshaw should be described. He asked if the officer would describe the accused as being mentally retarded, and the reply was, 'I would not go so far as to say that. I am not a mental expert. I should say he was slightly backward.' This became a grilling aimed at finding out how Ramshaw had been treated when questioned.

Lewis: 'I put it to you that he was a worn-out, tired man after the grilling by Sergeant Wolf and you?'

Davis: 'I was probably more worn-out myself.'

Lewis then referred to the showing of the scene of crime photos to Ramshaw, and made it seem like mental torture. Ramshaw had said that when he made his statement he was sandwiched between Davis and Wolf and was 'a nervous wreck'.

Lewis was out to show the jury that there was a possibility that the Yard men had used some tough tactics on a man with mental health problems. There had allegedly been provoking questions about a noose waiting for Ramshaw, and that a courting couple outside the house had heard him quarrelling with Emily. It is not difficult to picture the scene: two men applying tough and aggressive interrogation techniques to a man who is already distraught and weary, and becoming more and more confused as time goes on. The detective denied saying that 'the noose is getting tighter and tighter' to the accused, and denied mentioning strangling to torment him.

The final ploy by the defence was to tackle the question of Ramshaw's statement.

Lewis: 'Was the statement the result of questions put by you to the accused?'

Davis: 'No, Sir.'

Lewis: 'And of course, when you had got the answers, you had solved the riddle?'

Davis: 'No, Sir.'

Lewis: 'Why not?'

Davis: 'I was hoping to get corroborative evidence.'

Lewis: 'And have you got any?'

Davis: 'No.'

Lewis: 'And there is nothing in the statement which tells you how he committed the crime?'

Davis: 'No, Sir.'

Lewis knew that the prosecution case was cracking and was going for the most vulnerable and contentious element in the police officers' actions as reported by his client. It was not a difficult task, but it needed handling with care and sensitivity. He sensed the opposition in retreat.

The prosecution had to answer all this, and Mr Claxton for the Crown said that the statement was admissible and that under judges' rules it was possible to submit these things if a man was suspected. This refers to the written guidance given to police before the changes brought about by the Police and

Criminal Evidence Act of 1984. There was room for manoeuvre in these, and also room for exploitation and bias when there was a desperate urge to make an arrest. These rules were notoriously flexible, and could be adapted to suit anyone at any time with the right degree of resolve and teamwork.

But one aspect had not been touched on: Harry Ramshaw at work. Fred Cullen, of Ferry Road, worked with Ramshaw as a skip-filler at the Lysaghts company's works, and he confirmed that Ramshaw came to work just after 10 p.m. on the night of the murder. He had worked with Ramshaw all night, and left for home at around 5.40 a.m. What came out of this testimony was not only an alibi, but a perspective on Harry Ramshaw that added a great deal to an accurate picture of his personality being assembled in court. Cullen noted that Ramshaw was 'a quiet man and never joined in conversation in the cabin, and he was just the same as usual that night'. Harry Ramshaw was a man of regular habits and entirely reliable; he took cold tea to work in a pint bottle. On the night in question, he had behaved entirely normally. It was clear to everyone in the courtroom that Ramshaw would be cleared.

On 4 November, he was acquitted at Lincoln Assizes. The supposed 'confession' was totally discredited and Mr Justice Denning directed the jury with the words, 'You have no alternative. You must find this man not guilty.' What could be more simple and yet more telling than the fact that, in spite of the gargantuan struggle that had taken place in the kitchen, with the victim's blood in so many places, there had been no blood on any of Ramshaw's clothing, and no marks or signs of a fight on his body? He was the last person to see Emily alive, except the murderer, and that is all that could be said. Otherwise, his behaviour had been entirely in keeping with a man who had just lost his dearest friend, and there was no motive whatsoever for his killing her; it made sense to no-one. The man had an alibi, and there was no material evidence of his being in a tough physical confrontation.

In Lincoln this was a major attraction for the public, as the participation of the Scotland Yard men and the unresolved nature of the accused's mental condition had attracted the attention of the popular media. A very long queue had gathered in Lincoln waiting to enter the public gallery. The first stage of the events was that the all-male jury had to retire, as the depositions about the nature of the confession had to be stated and presented. A further addition to the defence case was an appraisal of Ramshaw by the prison medical officer, in which the opinion was expressed that the man 'had an intelligence which was below average – the equivalent of a child of eleven years and three months'. The issue was the procedure that took place before the interview with Ramshaw: here Ramshaw was told to take notes on what he saw before the detective saw him. Defence said that this might have had an effect on the man that it would not have had on a normal adult. The defence team had done an excellent job of work.

The judge expressed the central point of contention in this way: 'Confession or no confession the Crown must prove the case. If I had to disregard the evidence of the Chief Inspector I would find it difficult to know what he could say, except that there was no evidence upon which a jury could convict.' The result was that there was still only a minimal amount of detail known for sure about the scene of crime. All it came down to was that there had been a savage and merciless assault and murder, and then the body had been put in a pose that suggested some kind of sexual attack.

Finally we have to consider Harry Ramshaw. The man said that he went into the dock with a clear conscience. A reporter from the *Evening Telegraph* went with the news of the acquittal to his sister-in-law, Mrs Herbert Ramshaw, who lived in Newland Drive in Scunthorpe, and also to his sister Ida in Hull. The whole family had been through a traumatic time, and all had been convinced that he was innocent.

Harry's brother, Herbert, travelled back to Scunthorpe with him on a bus. It would have been a long, slow journey. They came home to a celebratory afternoon tea. His sister made a statement to the press: 'We never believed he was guilty, and his workmates and friends who had known him for years have said they would not believe it either, of a man like him.'

In the end, we have to look on the behaviour of the detectives with extreme suspicion and a certain amount of revulsion. What actually went on in the two interrogations will never be known, but all available opinions and reports suggest that the actions taken were grossly unfair when they were dealing with a man of Harry Ramshaw's limitations. There is a photograph that gives a triumphant closure to the saga of the Charlesworth case: it shows Harry with his brother and sister, smiling, as they sit together. In the picture, Harry is a small, quiet man; nothing suggests that he has been through hell, and that is not overstating the situation. We can only guess at what feelings went through him as he was subjected to the pressure of a 'grilling'. With hindsight, it is impossible to see why the investigation took the rather sinister turn it did, with the detectives deciding that applying some pressure would resolve things: it was a dangerous risk.

The case remains unsolved in the chronicles of Lincolnshire crime. Whoever the 'homicidal maniac' was, he was never traced. The entire unpleasant story of Emily Charlesworth's murder belongs to that number of cases in which circumstances dictate that a suspect has to be found, and the consequences were disastrous. From start to finish the murder case had been highly sensational and shrouded in mystery; the way it was reported provides an exemplar of the terrifying power of media amplification. As the result of this power the town thought there was a madman on the loose, and they were immediately frightened by any suspicious character in any one of the dozen town-centre pubs. The local press had reported the whole narrative of the killing and the hunt with astounding verve and enthusiasm; they reported well and accurately. The effect of this lively reporting was an exacerbation of the increasingly apprehensive atmosphere in the town, although great emphasis was placed on the likelihood that the 'maniac' had probably departed.

It is most ironical that so many rough and desperate characters were around the steel town at this time, and yet a harmless, child-like man was pulled in and charged, a man who never went out for a night of heavy drinking, who cared for his dearest friend and was cared for by her, and who worked hard in tough conditions. Justice was done in the end, and was patently seen to be done.

The Emily Charlesworth case has to go down as one of the three most prominent unsolved Scunthorpe murders of the last century. The other investigations had a fair amount of technology to back them up, and more sophisticated police strategies; the Charlesworth investigation was one in which the police team put on blinkers and overlooked some very obvious obstacles. Regarding the nature of the interviews with Ramshaw, we will never know the truth, but one ironical comment must be made. In the *Report of the Departmental Committee on Detective Work and Procedure* (1938) there is only one sentence concerning interviews with suspects in the main chapters; emphasis in this is on crime records, procedure, liaison and so on. The one reference to interviewing is this: '. . . that a man who has completed the course should have a good knowledge of criminal law and of court procedure, and what is more important, should have demonstrated . . . and have learned sound and systematic methods in the examination of a scene of crime, the questioning of witnesses . . .' One wonders what kind of skills were imparted to the officers in this case.

12

WHO KILLED THE BARTON RECLUSE?

Barton on Humber, 1969

The events of some unsolved murder cases have about them a sense of high drama: massive police manpower involved; pursuits and searches across barren tracts of land; media hype for weeks on end; myths about sightings of mysterious strangers. The story of how Robert Stephenson was killed contains all these elements. It is a cold case file with an emotional heat all its own when the historian opens the file yet again for a fresh look at the facts. The setting for the murder was a lonely farmhouse on a very quiet stretch of road between the ferry-crossing town of Barton on Humber and Barrow; it had the aspects of crime we associate with *film noir*: a night-time attack by two men desperate for money, men prepared to take a life for very little.

At his large and lonely house on the Barton–Barrow road in April 1969 Robert Stephenson lay gagged and wounded for several days, after a horrendous ordeal at the hands of two robbers who had struck him with iron bars and then callously left him to die. The 75-year-old had been shut up in one room with no food or water, and the house had been ransacked. He lasted long enough in hospital to say that his attackers spoke with Irish accents. They took only £8 and walked out into obscurity; despite a few leads at the time of the murder, the identity of the men who burst into his home and killed him remains a mystery.

Stephenson was a recluse who collected antiques and owned 51 acres of land in the area, as well as some property in Hull directly across the river. One of the main problems for the police at the time, as Detective Chief Inspector Bob Kirk told the papers in 1994 when he recollected the case, was that no-one knew exactly what objects had been kept in his home. Local rumours were that there were gold sovereigns and Dresden china. Certainly much was left in the house after the robbery, and it was later auctioned at Brigg Corn Exchange. On 18 October 1970 the hoard, much of which was coins, silver and jewellery, fetched around £1,000 – a large sum at the time.

Stephenson's home still stands, although in a ruined condition. (Evening Telegraph)

The case was reopened in 1989 after a 'tip-off' in the form of an anonymous telephone call. By that time the affair had become generally known as the Hermit Murder. The basic facts of the torture and the man's ordeal, the theft and the finding of the poor dying man by his neighbour, John Rigg, were known. The old man had been woken at midnight and battered on the head with iron bars. In the light of the phone call, new enquiries and fresh searches were made but to no effect. Rigg bought his neighbour's home in 1971.

At the time the enquiry escalated into a wide search across a huge area of north-east Lincolnshire; by 26 April, another group of twenty detectives were drafted into Barton, making a total of 120 men on the case. Detective Chief Inspector Joseph Camamile of Lincolnshire CID led the chase, and he had some details of two Irishmen they were looking for. The leads and connections led as far away as Berkshire and also to Harlesden, north London. The main lead was still the Irish reference of the dying man and sure enough, after identikits and other statements, there was a determined search locally for a 'rough-looking Irishman' who had called at a house 4 miles from Barton. He had been seen near Bonby Lodge after calling at Horkstow House to ask for food and drink.

A torchlight search was started across Saxby Wolds, and 15,000 people were interviewed. The Irishman had supposedly been seen running towards Horkstow Top. Check-points were set up and the police issued with flares. Camamile admitted that he had no definite connection, but noted that there must have been some reason for the man in question to run off. Officers were billeted in lodgings for considerable periods and they became a familiar sight around the historic little Humber ferry-crossing and rope-making town. Some were there for so long that they were not seen very often by their families in Scunthorpe or Grimsby.

The headquarters of the Barton manhunt was the focus of this large-scale operation. As the local paper pointed out, 'The top men from the CID were there,' including the Deputy Chief Constable, Albert Brown, who knew the area very well indeed. Thirty-nine men travelled from Grimsby and Scunthorpe every day, so the small town had to adapt sharply and provide for them; the cafes did very well and trade was brisk. The scale of the investigation was enormous but no breakthrough came.

Control Room, Barton. These detectives spent many weeks on site, away from home. (Evening Telegraph)

In the end we have a story of a heartless killing in an isolated area by two desperate men who were never caught. For several weeks groups of police officers covered the Barrow, New Holland and Barton areas but eventually to no avail. The story is, nevertheless, that of the central character – the victim. Stephenson was formerly a collector of second-hand clothes for a small business, and then his father left him money and property. He was worth £10,000 but had never signed a will; he was thought of as a harmless, timid eccentric who lived with his cat, Johnny. He was born in Barrow, but his parents had business interests in Hull for some considerable time. His elderly neighbours said that they did not see him at all for several months, as he was essentially a recluse. He was, they said, an intelligent man and always smartly dressed. His passion was to buy things that no-one else seemed to want, and to hoard them. I interviewed people about him for this book, and was told that when visitors came to his home they had to turn sideways in the hall to squeeze past high piles of books stacked against the walls.

The reporters of the time made much of Johnny; of course he was the only eye-witness to the attack. He eventually went to a Scunthorpe cattery where he was well cared for, and he certainly gained the status of a local celebrity during this enquiry.

Sergeant Blackwell, at the inquest, said, 'I don't know if they were Irish or Chinamen. They had iron bars.' The officer then said that the dying man commented that it had been a long time since any neighbour had been to see him, which points to the appeal at the heart of this case, the powerful mix of the inscrutability of the hermit and the puzzle of his brutal murder. The officer's laconic statement sums up much of the nature of this nasty and inhuman killing in the remote countryside. It was a very high profile case in the media and reporting went far and wide; the tabloids always provide vicarious thrills when such macabre crimes occur.

I interviewed officers who were involved in the enquiry at the time, hoping that meticulous detail might

Even though identikits of the two Irish suspects were circulated, no one was ever found and tried for the murder. (Evening Telegraph)

Police issue pictures

LINCOLNSHIRE police today issued identikit pictures of two men they wish to question in connection with the murder of 69-years-old Mr. Robert Stephenson, at Barton-on-Humber.

The men were seen in the Barton area between April 9 - 13.

Man No. 1 : 30 - 35 years, 5ft. 9in., stocky built, thick

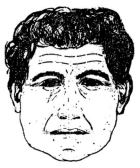

bushy ginger hair, combed forward over forehead; pock - marked complexion; believed wearing khaki battle-dress blouse under a fawn overcoat.

Man No. 2 : 35 - 40 years, height 5ft. 10in, to 6ft.,

medium build, dark hair brushed back, believed wearing a dirty fawn rain-coat.

Mr Stephenson. (Evening Telegraph)

lead to some fresh thought. One centrally important participant was John Olsson, who was actually in the ambulance with Robert Stephenson on the night. The journey must have been awful for him, as it entailed a rough ride on a B road along the side of the Humber to the nearest hospital at Scunthorpe. Olsson (a PC at the time) was in the police station at Barton on the afternoon that the news broke. He was stationed at North Ferriby nearby, but had called in at Barton to clean his moped.

Olsson left the house in the ambulance with Mr Stephenson at three minutes past five. He hoped to get a statement from him. A person who was thought to be dying could make a 'dying declaration', but he had to be aware he was close to death. John did not quite manage to get the old man to realise this. However, he did say that the attackers were Chinamen (something not brought out when the Irishmen were searched for but hinted at by the detective Blackwell, quoted above), that they were of dark complexion and had taken £3 from a piano. His speech was slurred. Olsson had of course to give a short report of what Stephenson said, but he tactfully left out the 'dying declaration' detail. In addition, Olsson told me there were some odd details at the scene of crime. The victim's braces were nailed to the piano, clearly indicating that the attackers had subjected the old man to sadistic terror and mental anguish. The handles on the door had been tied together by a belt. The room where he lay was stacked floor to ceiling with old newspapers. There was something dangling from the window – a belt, presumably used by the assailants to torture their victim. The entrance to the room had books stacked along the wall, leaving a small gap a person was just able to walk out of.

Stephenson used to go scavenging for materials on the tip in Hull, Olsson said; he once brought home a broken pair of binoculars, and said that with them he could look out of his back window and see a clock-tower in Hull. That a man with his wealth would do such things says a great deal about the kind of atmosphere he lived in: no real cleanliness and order, and plenty of eccentric behaviour. It was no wonder that the locals talked about him and knew his habits well.

Olsson's memories continued. He recalled how the enquiry started on 16 April, by which time an unfortunate rumour that Scotsmen had been caught and shot, replacing the Irish one. Olsson remembered Joe Camamile with affection; he used to live in a flat on Church Lane, and clearly had immense character and charisma.

There was a sighting of a Morris Oxford with peculiar plates; at the time everything that might be unusual was noted, of course. A notable turning point was the day when the focus changed to the pursuit of a tramp. Olsson and his colleagues walked from the A15 to the Ancholme (15 miles), looking for tramps. Another time, four officers went searching some brickyards for a tramp called Boston Jack. It was one among many leads that fizzled out. Every remark made about any lead worth pursuing was taken up. Olsson recalled one day when he was asked if anyone had been to see the air-raid shelter 'in the woods'. A man took him to some dug-outs that had been used by the Home Guard. There was a ladder leading down to a space where there had been bunk beds. The dug-outs were searched, along with every nook and cranny for miles around.

Harry Johnson was a constable at the time, and he recalled the beginning of the case. He answered the phone and was told to pack his suitcase, use his own car and report immediately to the hall at Barton. Harry pointed to a more practical side of such an investigation: a murder investigation, he said, meant lots of money going into the murder pot. 'In those days the police were always short of money but, in a murder investigation, the government almost always financed it.' He remembered the briefing in the hall at Barton, being crowded in with about fifty other officers. 'The victim had apparently died from head injuries. The main briefing was for organising and allocation of digs for the many policemen present.'

John Olsson, the officer in the ambulance. (Author's Collection)

From talking to officers who were actually involved in the hunt for the killers, it becomes obvious just how well known the victim's habits and character were around Barton. Harry's landlady knew 'about Mr Stephenson's house, habits, relatives, cuts of meat, and his political leanings'. In his opinion, if all the policemen lodged around the area had learned as much about Stephenson as he had done, then the murder would have been solved in a few days. Harry gives us an insight into the procedure for such a murder hunt: 'I was given a large pile of pro-formas, one to be completed for every house, farm, and then one for each resident of these.' The territory covered was 'compassed between the Humber in the north to Brigg in the south, and between Scunthorpe in the west and Immingham in the east.' They were given large-scale maps, and smaller areas were allotted to each officer. The aim was to work fast across all this land and get information to the murder room very swiftly. Any place they could not enter was noted, and a follow-up team would go there later. It was a long and exhausting task: 'The river Ancholme totally bisected our area from the Humber to Brigg with no old bridges in between, which added more and more miles and time.'

Memoirs and anecdotes like these fill in some of the missing dimensions of this major case. It was a massive hunt, expensive as well as extensive, fuelled by rumours. Any stranger was suspect and anything unfamiliar was noticed and studied. Another local told me about a hunt for a character nicknamed 'Lumpy Neck'. For a while he was a definite target for enquiries: in the absence of a definite suspect, he was at least someone who needed to be questioned and eliminated. It was a typical example of media amplification; anything slightly grotesque or suspicious suddenly became newspaper fodder, along with statements by psychics and prophetic dreams. Another supposed lead was the sighting of two men hopping on to a lorry. The subsequent strenuous efforts to stop lorries and search them came to nothing.

The only sure thing was that whoever had committed this awful murder had accents that were not of the Barton area. In his confused state, with concussion and some brain damage, Robert Stephenson could only describe the accents of his two attackers as foreign. After that he guessed, which only led to further guesswork and speculation.

The Stephenson case was also one which illustrated the tendency at that time to take a special interest in the mechanics of police work. The local newspapers carried detailed accounts of such things as the incident room, set up at Barton police station, and their pictures showed officers from Grimsby and Scunthorpe manning the phones.

Harry Johnson's words probably sum up the feelings of many professionals involved in this case: 'After three weeks of enquiries our work was done. We had contacted, face to face, and extracted information from every adult living within 150 square miles. Our last job, therefore, before going home, was to thank Mrs Goodwin [their landlady] with a bunch of flowers and a box of chocolates. My only regret was that Mr Stephenson's killer was still at liberty.' As he also pointed out, all this was going on in the pre-computer age, with no DNA and so on. There have been perhaps ten unsolved cases in Lincolnshire in the last century which have been written about fairly widely and extensively; but this one of the sad death of the Barton recluse is particularly prominent for its sombre nature, taking place in a lonely, flat stretch of north Lincolnshire, by the Humber, that the poet Philip Larkin calls 'the end of England'.

As with so many unsolved murders, the only option left is to speculate on potential suspects, people with possible motives, any known enemies and so on. But these categories were naturally pursued actively at the time. The old man was easily noticeable, moving around at sales and markets in the local area, and his habitation was vulnerable to say the least. None of the many reports given in the press, as the investigation continued, deals with any serious suspect or motive other than the obvious conclusions drawn from the robbery itself. The killers very likely thought that there was a massive stash of wealth somewhere in the building, and the nailed braces and the nature of the violence against Mr Stephenson suggest that they were trying to extort some information about this from him. Apparently they failed, and it cost him his life, but then, he claims, they said they were going to kill him anyway.

It was a brutally heartless murder of a gentle old man. He was often seen on his bicycle, as I was told by former constable Charles Watkinson, who knew the victim as a familiar sight around Barton. Bicycling was entirely in keeping with the man's habits, for he would not have thought spending money on cars and petrol was worthwhile. He also regularly attended the local auctions and markets, and it seems odd now that he was not an integral part of the 'county set' who took antiques seriously and went about it in a convivial way; he was a loner, hence his vulnerability.

As one officer said to me: 'Turning away from a murder case is maybe the worst feeling for a police officer. The sense of failure is unbearable.' If it is any comfort, even Sherlock Holmes would probably have struggled with this one. Such was the media interest, and so long did the investigation last, that the newspapers turned their attention rather more on Mr Stephenson's cat, Johnny, and a campaign was started to make sure he was given an acceptable new home. The officers involved must have felt they were leaving what we would now call a 'media circus' rather than an unsolved police case.

13

A MISCELLANY

MURDER OF THE RECTOR, 1602

In September 1602 Francis Cartwright spoke out loudly in the market place at Market Rasen against the rector of Aisthorpe, William Storr. Cartwright was in a passion of hatred because Storr had interposed in a noisy dispute about rights of common, and this had happened after the evening service on a Sunday, and in the house of God, no less. Cartwright was well off and the son of one of the 'lords of the town', as a later account put it. He was of the opinion that the churchman needed to be taught a lesson. Storr had been born in Aisthorpe and was a Fellow of Corpus Christi College. He was given the living of Market Rasen in 1597. He was keen and enthusiastic, and perhaps rather too haughty, but he did not deserve the treatment he was to get from his young enemy. When Cartwright ranted in the market place he called Storr 'A scurvie, lousy, paltry priest: that whoever said he was his friend was a rogue and a rascal . . .'

In the market, Cartwright said he would cut Storr's throat and hang his quarters on the maypole. The natural response from the rector was to try to restrain the man, so he moved to have the magistrate act against him, but this ploy failed and the feud escalated. The priest began to preach on Sodom and Gomorrah, with clear references to some of the rowdy and violent locals, including young Cartwright, who believed that the priest was on the side of the common people against the landlord class. It was noted that Cartwright listened to this sermon and watched the rector generally around the town, then seemed to 'note diligently with his pen' the words against him.

A week later, as Storr was walking to the south of Market Rasen, he was viciously set upon by Cartwright, who slashed at him with his sword and left him for dead. Indeed, the rector was mortally wounded and died shortly after. It was an agonising death; he was taken to a house nearby and then visited by a surgeon and a bone-setter. The description of his wounds in the pamphlet about the case has this account: 'he had a gash on the outside of the left thigh to the very bone; and again on the left knee, his leg being bended as he lay, he [Cartwright] cut him the fashion and compass of an horse-shoe, battering in pieces the whirl-bone [knee-cap]'. It was no problem for the local powers to sort out who was the killer, and Cartwright was taken to a magistrate.

The market place in Market Rasen. (Laura Carter)

But justice was not seen to be done, for he was given 'a very slender bail' and left town. Having a high status, he worked to obtain a pardon, and clearly all would have been well for him had it not been for the widow of the rector, who persisted with the prosecution. For five years she pursued the case and objected to the man's pardon, even though the king, James I, was in support of this appeal. Historians have speculated on exactly what position and influence the killer had. We know that he had property in the glebe of the vicarage, a draper's shop on the market place. If he was one of the Cartwright family of Normanby, then he had strong clannish support in times of trouble.

Later in life, however, the killer wrote his autobiography; here we seem to have another personality entirely. Cartwright's life was still most eventful, however. He was once attacked by four men and almost killed, but he lived to quarrel another day and in a scrap killed another man, a certain William

Three Bloodie Murders

The first, committed by *Francis Cartwright* vpon *William Storre*, M[r]
Art, Minifter and P[r]eacher at *Market Raifin* in the countie of *Lincolne*.

The Second, committed by *Elizabeth Iames*, on the body of her Mayde, i[n]
Parifh of *Egham* in *Surrie* : who was condemned for the fame fa[c]t at Sai[d]
Margarets hill in Southwark, the 2. of Iuly 1613, and lieth in the Whi[te] L[io]r
till her deliuerie : difcouered by a dombe Mayde, and a Dogge.

The Third, committed vpon a Stranger, very lately, neere *High-gate* foure mi[les]
from *London* : very ftrangely found out by a Dogge alfo, the 2. of Iuly. 1613

'Three Bloodie Murders', from an old pamphlet. (Author's Collection)

Riggs of Fulbeck. But among all this trouble he married and wrote about his life. He repented of his murder of the rector, and claimed that he had only ever intended to wound him slightly. But that is hardly supportable when we note that Cartwright was still having fights when he went to sea, serving under Sir Richard Hawkins; there was such a fear that he would have been sentenced to death by a court martial that he constantly changed jobs and addresses.

The last we know of him is that he fell from a coach and almost died.

PAPIST MURDERER, 1682

A Protestant pamphlet of 1683 tells of a killing by a Roman Catholic in Kyme in 1682, and the occasion is used for an unhealthy indulgence in religious rhetoric and hatred. The pamphlet makes a great deal of the 'powerful temptation of Satan' that led the farmer, Sherburn, to kill his wife. It goes on, 'What inducements the Devil made use of to tempt him to this horrid villainy is yet unknown.'

What happened was that Sherburn attacked his wife for no apparent reason as she lay in bed. He 'throttled or suffocated her, and by trampling upon her, and many furious blows upon her stomach and bowels, beat the breath out of her body and killed her'. After that, with a puzzling lack of direction in what he should do next (such as hiding or destroying her body), Sherburn went to sleep in another bedroom. At the time, of course, his own people in the Catholic Church had to look for a reason in this apparent madness: was he distressed rather than possessed? They alleged, says the pamphlet, that he was 'distempered in his mind when a youth of twenty years . . .'

Naturally there was no other recourse than to have the man taken before a magistrate and then imprisoned in Lincoln Castle for trial. He was condemned, and it is difficult to see any other interpretation than the fact that he was not in possession of his rational faculties. After all, he left his wife's body in the bed, and never tried to fabricate any other tale that would have involved supposed killers, such as robbers or vagrants. The author of the pamphlet makes it sound as though he had no belief in the possibility of the man's 'distraction'. In such social contexts, when men still believed in occult answers to some tough questions, it is plain to see where the attitudes behind this hatred come from.

FALDINGWORTH GATE HIGHWAYMEN, 1733

In the chronicles of crime, told in the pages of The *Newgate Calendar* (1773), there are several stories told of highwaymen on the Great North Road and in such wild places as the Moor Fields or Epping Forest (where Dick Turpin began his life of villainy), but only one of these involves Lincolnshire men.

The Bloody Papist:

Or, a True

RELATION

Of the Horrid and Barbarous

MURDER

Committed by one *Ro. Sherburn* of *Kyme* in *Lincolnſhire*, (a Noː
torious P A P I S T,) upon his Wife, whom in an Inhumane
Manner he Murder'd in her *Bed*, for which he is now a
Priſoner in *Lincoln-Goal*.

Amongſt all the grievous and Raigning Sins too frequently
Committed amongſt us, That of *Murther*, as it is one of
the *deepeſt dye*, and moſt unnatural,ſo it deſerves the ſtrictː
eſt Diſquiſition, and not only *Cries* loud to Heaven for *Vengeance*,
but alſo to Gods *Vicegerents* on Earth, for exact and ſpeedy *Juſtice* to
be inflicted on thoſe that are Guilty of it. To kill any Unlawfully,
is no leſs than an Aſſault upon God in Effigie, a Defacing of the
Divine Image : but when ſuch a Barbarous Crime ſhall be aggra-
vated with Deſign and Premeditation , and ſuch a Circumſtance
as this,that'tisActed againſt ſo near a Relation as is the ſame *Fleſh*,
and whom, both the Laws of God and man, the Dictates of *Reaː*
ſon,and a mans own Solemn *Vows*, had in a ſpecial manner obligʼd
him toDefend, Love, and Cheriſh,it ſwells beyond all Proportion
of Ordinary Impiety, and grows monſtrouſly Deteſtable.

This *Ro. Sherburn* livʼd at a Village callʼd *Kyme* in *Lincolnː*
ſhire; his Trade or Occupation, a *Farmer* or Dealer in Cattel ; and
by Profeſſion of Religion, a *Papiſt* ; whether he were bred up ſo
from his Infancy, or ſince Revolted and Apoſtatizʼd thereunto,
we have not been able to Learn; 'Tis certain that for diverſe years
paſt he has ownʼd himſelf of that Perſwaſion, and very Zealous
and Obſtinate therein ; and as to his Life and Converſation,it was
ſuitable enough to the Principles of their Mock-Religion ; It beː
ing nothing ſtrange that thoſe whom God hath ſo far forſaken as
to give them up to believe *a Lie* (for *Popery* in the whole Body
of it is no other)ſhould likewiſe be left without *Natural Affections*,
and abandon themſelves to *Work all kind of Wickedneſs with Greedi-*
neſs.

He had long been married (by Report in the Country near 20
years,) to an honeſt Loving and Induſtrious Woman, and to the
outward view of the World they ſeemʼd to live very agreeably toː

A   gethe

'The Bloody Papist'. This tract shows the hatred and distrust of Catholics at
the time. (Lincolnshire Library)

A highwayman. (Laura Carter)

The rogues in question were two brothers, Isaac and Thomas Hallam, and they plied their nasty trade around Market Rasen in the early eighteenth century. They were notorious, and so threatening in the area that a reward was offered for their capture.

Of all their heartless crimes, their murder of a post-boy is the most documented and appears to have had the most effect in Lincolnshire. They must have had a brutal and sadistic element in their nature, for the tale is told that they took hold of the post-boy, William Wright, and almost cut his head from his body; he was found in that bloody state in a post-chaise at Faldingworth Gate. He had been robbed and the carriage was saturated with his blood. They also grabbed another boy and told him that he had to blow his horn, and that this would be his 'death knell'. His throat was cut, and, shockingly, they also cut the throat of his horse. The repercussions were that expressions of public disgust were expressed: in Lincoln the post-boys gathered and blasted the peace with their horns, to make people notice and think about what was happening. 'One of them was observed to weep', says the *Calendar* writer.

The search for them began in earnest, and it took a month to find them. When the brothers were tracked down and convicted of two murders they certainly did not accept their fate; they somehow found a case-knife, which they turned into a saw, and cut off their chains in Lincoln Castle. With a spike-nail they started hacking at the cell wall, but were discovered. At trial they confessed to an additional sixty-three robberies and a great deal of violence, done 'with mere wantonness', and their fate was sealed.

The Hallams were to be executed at the place where they had killed the post-boy, Wright. The record says that Isaac, coming to that place, 'fell into violent agonies and perturbation of mind'. They were both hanged, and one of them 'shrieked in a dreadful manner, the other praying fervently'. They were deprived of their lives on 20 February 1733, and the roads around Market Rasen became much safer for travellers. This all happened at a time when highway robbery was fashionable and attracted villains with a sense of style and fashion, like a young man about this time who dressed in a greatcoat, had a star painted on his head and wore a bob in his hair. He was active just a few miles away near Brigg, but he did not kill anyone, as far as we know. Other strange robbers would be so desperate to be highwaymen that they would use a candlestick to hold up a coach. There were plenty of amusing tales around at the time, in the Dick Turpin tradition, but there was nothing funny about the Hallams and certainly nothing gentlemanly: they were brutal killers and died as violently as they had lived.

IRISH LABOURERS FALL OUT, 1831

On a farm near Lincoln Thomas Sewards and his son-in-law, Michael Lundy, were working for a farmer, doing some seasonal work for him. They were heaping and burning weeds in the July of this year, and after they had eaten their evening meal, the farmer offered them his barn for the night, as they were due to start work again very early the next day. The farmer, Wilson, saw that Sewards was not well, and he put out some straw and sacks for the two Irishmen, also giving them a key so they could secure themselves inside for the night, if they wished.

Sewards could not speak English, but he was not well, and Wilson negotiated with Lundy. As time went on and evening came the two men were in the barn. At about 8 p.m., Lundy was sitting outside by a carpenter's bench, surrounded by the man's tools. This was a long way from the Wilsons' farmhouse, and all seemed well, but an hour later, as Mrs Wilson was feeding poultry, she heard a cry of murder and saw Lundy, only half-dressed, seeming to be crazed and ranting.

Lundy then told a long and far-fetched account of being accosted by 'a tall black man, six feet high with a broad-brimmed hat' who asked him if he wanted some company, and he had supposedly insisted that he sleep with the labourer. Lundy even claimed that he had had a fight and been pelted with stones. Mrs Wilson did see that there was a swelling on his forehead, seeming to confirm that story. But when the Wilsons went to investigate the situation at the barn they were understandably shocked at the horrendous sight that met their eyes as they walked inside.

There was Sewards, with the carpenter's axe buried in his face, down to the mouth; there was also a wound on his scalp. Lundy continued screaming and muttering prayers, not daring to go near the body.

The Wilsons naturally set no credence on the tale of the tall black man and carried Lundy off to a constable at Elthorpe; the body was then taken there on a cart. It soon became apparent that Lundy had been in a fight; there was blood sprinkled on his trousers and coat, and he had washed his hands, which contrasted with their very dirty state that the Wilsons had observed earlier. On investigation, the constable found the imprint of a naked foot by a pond close by, and when the man was searched 6s was found on him. The Wilsons said that when they had first met the Irishmen they had seemed quiet and peaceable.

Lundy, after this murderous rage, became yet another client for the hangman at Cobb Hall, Lincoln Castle.

MURDER ON THE BOSTON ROAD, 1833

The printer in Silver Street, Lincoln, was out to exploit the hunger for crime stories in the general public, and William Taylor's imminent execution was a perfect example of the genre of the broadsheet murder story. The story, on one sheet, was adorned with a drawing of the 'new drop' at Cobb Hall, and there was a ballad, stressing the horrible deed the villain had done on the Boston road:

> Several heavy blows he struck him, all on his head and side,
> Not time to make his peace with God before he groaned and died

The victim in question was William Burbank, who had been playing cards with the killer in a beer shop at Heckington on 9 March 1833. Burbank had a lot of cash on him on that occasion, and he went to the counter to buy beer, with 'twenty or thirty shillings' in his purse. Taylor was in the room with the other drinkers. He was from Heckington, son of a carrier working between Sleaford and Boston. Although he was supposedly well respected and father of three children, he had a wild younger brother. Something of that wildness was to emerge in William on this night. Burbank's friends knew about the purse and the money, and Burbank was heard to say that he was going home to clean up and have a shave. He left and, about half an hour later, Taylor left the beer house too.

A wine merchant called Nicholls found Burbank's body on the road the next morning at 5.45. A stake was lying near it, but Nicholls was observant enough

A Full, true and particular account of William Taylor, the unfortunate man who was Executed on the New Drop at Lincoln, on Monday the 18th March, 1833, for the wilful Murder of William Burbank, on the road from Sleaford to Boston, on Saturday the 9th March instant.

Give ear unto this horrid tale, good people far and near,
And of a barbarous murder, you presently shall hear,
Committed was on Sleaford road, the truth I will unfold;
A more cold blooded murder, scarce ever yet was told,

In Heckington one W. Taylor the murderer did dwell,
And likewise W. Burbanks, who by his hand has fell,
They had been drinking and gambling, its true what I impart,
And all that time this monster, had murder in his heart.

With cudgel in possession to Burbank then he came,
And stopped him on the road, his hands in blood to stain,
Several heavy blows he struck him, all on his head and side,
Not time to make his peace with God before he groaned & died.

To see the blood in streams to flow from Burbank's head,
You'd think it almost impossible so much for him to have bled,
But soon the villain was taken, and placed in a dreary cell,
For murdering poor Burbank as many a tongue can tell.

Now when his trial did come on, he at the bar did stand,
Like Moses he stood waiting, for the holy Lord's command,
The Judge when passing sentence made him this reply,
You're guilty of the murder, so prepare yourself to die.

You must prepare yourself to die, on Monday on the tree,
When hung the usual time thereon, buried you must be,
May these few lines a warning be, and prove to others good,
That they may ever shun the sin, of spilling precious blood.

William Taylor, aged 21, late of Heckington, laborer, charged by the Coroners inquest with the wilful murder of William Burbank, on the highway between Heckington and Sleaford, in the County of Lincoln.

William Brown keeps a beer shop at Heckington near Sleaford, the prisoner W. Taylor, W. Burbank, B. Medley, W. Nash and W. Cock, were at his house on Saturday the 9th day of March, W. Burbank came to witness house about half past two o'clock in the afternoon, he played two or three games at cards with the before mentioned W. Nash, W. Cock, and B. Medley, about 4 o'clock Burbank asked witness wife told him it was somewhere about 4 o'clock, Burbank the deceased took out his purse to pay for two pints of ale, which he had lost, and said that he wanted to get shaved and then call that part of the town over as he went home, and immediately went out of the house; witness should know the purse again, it appeared to have about 20 or 30 shillings in it, the prisoner also saw the purse, prisoner remained about half an hour in the house after the deceased had left it, the rest of the party remained in the house until the prisoner returned about 7 o'clock in the evening. Prisoner said he would make one to play at cards for a quart, played 3 games, on the last game he said he would bet three pence on his game, he would have three pence for the ale, and said he would then go home. The prisoner remained until about nine o'clock, and was then taken into custody. Witness went on the following Monday morning, to a place called the scalp house in the church to see a dead body, it was the body of W. Burbank.

John Nichols is a Wine and Spirit Merchant, residing at Sleaford, he left Heckington on Saturday the 9th of March, to go to Sleaford at a quarter before six o'clock in the evening, about a mile and a quarter from Heckington he observed the body of a man laying on the road, he dismounted and went up to it, he lifted one hand up with his stick, the man appeared to be dead, but was quite warm, supposed it might have been an accident, but on turning round he observed a stake laying across the hedge, one end of which was very bloody, it was five or six yards from the body, it was day light, the stake could not have been taken from the adjoining hedge on which it was laying, witness has seen the stake since in possession of the constable of Heckington, witness immediately rode back to Heckington for Mr. Gibbs, a surgeon, they returned to the body together.

Isaac Cooper, is a rag gatherer, lives at Heckington, on Saturday the 9th inst. he went to Mr. Arnold's Mill near Heckington church, about half past five o'clock in the afternoon, met the prisoner W. Taylor, against the gate of the close in which the Mill stands, witness asked prisoner where he was going to at that time of night, prisoner said he did not know exactly just then, but afterwards said he was going a shepherding, prisoner was going Sleaford way, witness afterwards met W. Burbank about 40 yards after the prisoner, witness spoke to him, he appeared to be very little in liquor, was also going Sleaford way. Witness has since seen a dead body, it was the body of W. Burbank.

W. Hilton, is a carpenter at Heckington, left home on Saturday the 9th inst. about six o'clock to go a shepherding, to a close by the side of the turnpike road, leading from Heckington to Sleaford, he met the prisoner W. Taylor a little past six o'clock, a short distance from Heckington town end. Prisoner asked witness if he could tell him of a job. Witness knows Hilton's close, it is fenced with a quick hedge, it is three quarters of a mile from Heckington, part of the hedge is newly plashed, there are several loose stakes.

W. Gibbs, is a surgeon, residing at Heckington, Mr. Nichols came for witness shortly after six o'clock, on Saturday the 9th inst. to go with him to a place on the Sleaford road, where he found the body of a dead man, it was W. Burbank, examined the body, it was quite warm, and witness supposes it had not been dead more than quarter of an hour, the skull was fractured, a hole into which witness could get his finger, was perforated through the forehead into the brain, the lower part of the forehead was likewise destroyed, the nose was divers quite from its proper direction, the bones of which were literally crushed to atoms, the lip was hanging down in a flap, the upper jaw was fractured, the back part of the head was out, by blows from a round instrument, deceased died from the

effects of those wounds, a large hedge stake is a likely instrument to cause such wounds. Witness was present when prisoner was apprehended, he denied his guilt. When the constable was going to lock prisoner up for the night, prisoner said he would tell all he knew about it, the prisoner said the purse was to be found near the spot where the body was found, on the other side of the road nearer to Heckington, the blood on the hedge stake was quite fresh, it was wet.

Charles Mastin is a Coroner for the County of Lincoln, and lives at Boston, he committed the prisoner, took the prisoner's examination, and cautioned him that any thing which prisoner might say would be brought as evidence against him. Mr. Mastin was sworn to his signature, and the deposition of the prisoner was put in and read, it was to the following effect: that the prisoner and the deceased were walking on the road together, the deceased began to quarrel with prisoner about the cards and struck prisoner with his stick, prisoner returned the blow, deceased again struck the prisoner, prisoner then knocked deceased down and struck him two or three times, took from him his purse, emptied it of its contents, 2s. 7d. then threw the purse by the other side of the road, Burbank was not then dead, prisoner returned to Heckington, and on his way met W. Hilton, (as stated in Hilton's evidence above,) then went to the beer shop kept by W. Brown and played two or three games at cards, (as stated by that witness.)

J. Wilton is a Cooper, and lives at Heckington, went to the place where the murder was committed and a short distance from it and on the opposite side of the road he found a purse which he gave to John Robinson, chief constable of Sleaford.

Robert Squire is the constable of Heckington, and produced a bludgeon, which he had received from Mr. Gibbs a Surgeon. The bludgeon was a piece of white thorn about four feet long, and about the thickness of a man's wrist, the back of one end was all bruised off and covered with blood, near the end a part of a branch remained, about three inches long, and as thick as a finger, which accounts for the hole through the forehead into the brain, (as stated in the surgeon's evidence.)

John Robinson, is a constable of Sleaford, and produced a purse, which he received from J. Wilton. W. Brown, the keeper of the beer shop, is then recalled, who swears that it is the identical purse, which he saw in the possession of W. Burbank, on the afternoon of Saturday, the 9th instant.

Mr. Gibbs, being recalled, stated that the wounds he had before described might be caused by the bludgeon now producing by the constable Squire, into whose possession witness gave it — The Squire, being asked who the prisoner attempted to shake the crime off himself and put it on to others, he replied yes, the prisoner told him that he was innocent of the murder himself, but he could tell them who it was that had done it.

This was the case for the prosecution. The Learned Judge, then addressed the Jury at considerable length, recapitulating every minute circumstance that was given in evidence relative to this dreadful affair, making suitable comments as he proceeded in order to make every thing as plain and intelligible as possible, the gentlemen of the Jury appeared to pay every attention, and after recalling some of the witnesses to enquire into some trifling matters that did not appear exactly plain, and a few minutes consultation they through their Foreman with a down cast look, and a faltering tongue, pronounced a verdict of GUILTY; the Proclamation being delivered the Learned Judge proceeded to pass the awful sentence of Death on the prisoner, who maintained a sullen silence, his lordship addressed the prisoner at considerable length in an eloquent and solemn manner, commenting on the clearness of the evidence, the magnitude of the crime being the greatest that one man can commit against his fellow man, and concluding by beseeching the prisoner to make the best use of the short time allowed him by law, to obtain pardon of his just and merciful God, through the merits of our Saviour Jesus Christ. He then sentenced him to be hanged, on Monday the 18th March instant, and his body to be buried within the precincts of the prison.

William Taylor was a native of Heckington near Sleaford, he has a father living, who has for many years followed the occupation of a carrier, between the Towns of Sleaford, Heckington, and Boston, he bears an unimpeachable character for steadiness and sobriety, and is greatly respected by all who know him, we understand he has or rather had three sons, the elder of whom is we understand a very steady, excellent young man, in fact quite a religious character, the subject of this brief sketch, and his younger brother have for a considerable time led a life of dissipation, and have been almost a terror to the neighbourhood in which they lived.

EXECUTION.—The unfortunate man was conducted from his dreary cell and handed to the Executioner. Being pinioned he was conducted to the place of execution, where he suffered the awful penalty of the Law in the presence of a great number of Spectators, at the appointed time.

Leary, Printer, Silver Street, Lincoln.

An execution broadsheet, a sensational example of popular crime literature of this time.
(Author's Collection)

to see that it had not been taken from a fence nearby. He took the body to a surgeon at Heckington, and a constable went to the scene, taking hold of the stake. Taylor had certainly been rash in his actions: two witnesses had met him that night and said so in court later; a rag-gatherer, Isaac Cooper, also met him and asked where Taylor was going so late at night. He received no definite answer. A man called Hilton who was a carpenter, was doing some shepherding work early in the day and he too saw Taylor. He also saw that there were several loose stakes in the place where Taylor was seen standing.

Poor Burbank had been attacked with real fury: the surgeon, Gibbs, reported that the skull was fractured and that there was a hole in the forehead; his nose had been squashed flat and the bones totally crushed. His jaw had been broken and the large stake was the most likely weapon. When Taylor was arrested there was no attempt to make up a story; he came clean and revealed that the purse, which had been the reason for the attack, was lying at the spot where he killed Burbank. The rest of the story then came out in Taylor's statement. He said that the two of them had walked together and fallen out; they had argued about the earlier gambling at the beer house. Taylor said that Burbank had provoked him, hitting him with his stick, and that in retaliation he had knocked the man to the ground. The surgeon's evidence and the examination of the stake (the 'bludgeon' as it was called) led to one conclusion. The judge apparently spent some time sermonising on what had happened in a solemn tone, and then everyone present waited for the foreman of the jury to speak.

The broadsheet writer noted that the foreman had a downcast look and spoke falteringly as he said 'Guilty', so the judge sentenced the prisoner to be hanged on Monday, 18 March, 'and his body to be buried within the precincts of the prison'. His last moments of life, as he walked from his miserable cell, were spent with massive crowds looking at him, as he was the centre of attraction for that day. It seems that the expected speech and repentance were not forthcoming.

MURDER OF A GAMEKEEPER, 1839

William Dadley was a young man from Aylsham in Norfolk who came to Lincolnshire and worked for Captain Mansell at Well Hall, near Alford. The prospects for a new life seemed good, and he married at St Botolph's Church in Boston in January 1839, his wife being Margaret Brown. They planned to settle in a gamekeeper's house near Ulceby Cross. He was to work the area as head gamekeeper for a Member of Parliament, Robert Christopher. There he was, just married, and with a bright future to look forward to. The wedding celebrations began with a party on 10 January, but as the guests were having a good time shots were heard out in the woods, and Dadley felt he had to go and investigate.

Baker's destination, Port Arthur, Tasmania. (Author's Collection)

Strangely, though, he went out into the night unarmed, although he did take a man with him, Charles Harrison. There was a serious poaching problem on the estate; there had been recent prosecutions and the perpetrators sent to a house of correction, and some men had been given prison sentences also. On this night the young married man tracked down the poachers, but one of them turned on him and shot him dead.

There was one obvious suspect: a desperate character called John Baker from Partney, who was linked in some people's minds to another killing of a gamekeeper at Normanby. He had a reputation in the area for being a rebel and a dangerous man. There was a strenuous effort made to bring in Dadley's killer, and a reward was offered in the hope that someone would turn in the man responsible. All roads of enquiry did indeed lead to Baker, and he was arrested and charged, being hunted down to a village not far off and cornered in a loft with a gun in his hand. Baker was faced with burglary charges as well, and was taken to Lincoln for trial. There was no definite evidence to convict him of the Dadley murder but he was convicted of serious theft charges and his death sentence was commuted to transportation, as so many were at that time.

There is no certainty that Baker killed the young husband. It is not difficult to imagine the feelings about the sad affair in the area, and the headstone in the Well churchyard says something of this: it notes that Dadley was 'hurried into his Redeemer's presence by the hand of a murderer, in the 32nd. Year of his age . . .' There is even a memorial stone in the place where he was shot, saying simply, 'W. Dadley murdered by poachers on this spot, 10 January, 1839.'

MOTHER KILLS CHILD, 1844

The *Lincolnshire Chronicle* for 2 August 1844 relates the sad tale of a 31-year-old woman who walked to the scaffold and paused as she did so to 'bid a lingering farewell to the bright world which she had sacrificed'. She was wearing a black dress and carried a prayer book; some said that her features had an expression of ghastly agony. The massive crowd gathered as usual, everyone jostling to find a good spot for watching the high drama of the hanging. They would have seen the all-too-familiar procession of prisoner, chaplain, bailiffs and hangman. The man with the unpleasant task of seeing that she was hanged as quickly as possible was William Calcraft, the national executioner. One reporter said, 'The effect of her appearance on the immense crowd was awfully striking – a profound stillness reigned through the living mass.'

What had she done to deserve this? Eliza Joyce had poisoned her son William, as well as her daughter Ann and her step-daughter Emma. She confessed to these crimes in Boston workhouse, telling the master about it, and this was after she and her husband had separated. She had married

William Joyce, being his second wife, in Boston in 1840, and they had lived an ordinary life. But after giving birth to William and finding that he was very weak and sickly, she had been immersed in what today we would call a puerperal depression. This is evident from her later explanations about what she had done. She bought some arsenic although her husband had not wanted her to, as he feared her reasons for buying it were not for use against pests. (At this time there were no controls against its purchase.) He found out that she had been given arsenic instead of nux vomica, and then he realised that half of the packet she bought was missing. The boy William was then seriously sick with all the signs of arsenic poisoning.

He made a statement about the poison and the illness, and Eliza was arrested. Her son died that Christmas, 1842. At the Summer Assizes she was acquitted, as there was doubt about whether or not the whole business had been accidental. In her confession in the workhouse the first killing, of her baby girl, was weighing heavily on her conscience and she told the tale of how she had bought three pennyworth of laudanum and given it to little Emma, who had died quickly. She said plaintively, in explanation of this, when the workhouse master asked her why she had done these awful things, 'I don't know, except I thought it was such a troublesome thing to bring a family of children into this troublesome world.' Her emotional state, and her husband's fears about the arsenic, become understandable when he noted that she said that she was 'so burdened that she could not live, and hoped that, as she had confessed, she should be better'.

In her third trial in Lincoln in 1844 she was charged with two murders. She had basically been afraid of having a large family and all the responsibility and travail that went with that condition.

That was the route to the gallows; Calcraft adjusted the rope and as the bell Old Tom chimed midday she fell into eternity; she died, the press reported, without a struggle. Eliza Joyce was the last woman in England to be hanged for a murder to which she had confessed and pleaded guilty.

A STRANGE LAST REQUEST, 1893

A mariner from the port of Grimsby, waiting for execution in Lincoln prison, wanted to get something off his chest. It was a confession of a crime he had done that was nothing to do with the reason he was in the execution cell. It was a story of him ramming and sinking a fishing boat of a company that was competing with another man's. He had never said anything about this to anyone; he had been paid well for the nasty work.

Henry Rumbold, thirty-seven, was a captain of a fishing smack working from Grimsby. He was married but was fond of other female company, and that was not hard to find around the docks. He started spending time with a woman thirteen years younger than him, Harriet Rushby. The skipper was

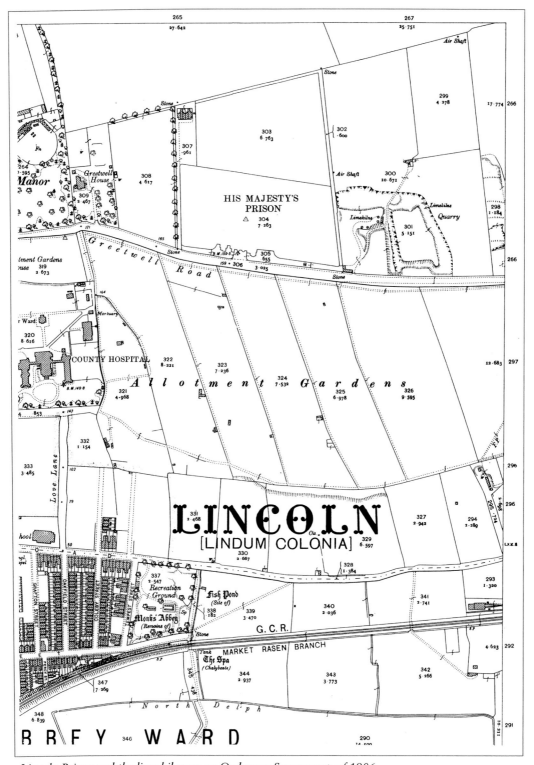

Lincoln Prison and the lime kilns on an Ordnance Survey map of 1906.

not simply after a rough time with a lady of the night, however. He tried to play what we might now call a 'sugar daddy' role but with a touch of dignity.

He thought that Harriet, if she were to be available to him when he was back from sea and he wanted some entertainment outside the marriage bed, should be well housed and looked after. He provided her with somewhere to lodge. But it wasn't enough for her: she felt the exciting pull of the pubs and the musical entertainments too much. She also liked spending time with a variety of men. When he came home and went to visit she was not there, and never had been.

This is a tale of possession. Rumbold wanted to add her to his list of property. He perhaps thought that a man with some status should have a mistress, and a decent one. When she didn't turn out to be the woman he wanted he took it into his head to go looking for her, and with a gun in his hand. He searched the streets and eventually found her with a crowd. He had the gun out and was raging; she was grabbed and taken into the upstairs room of her lodging house. Rumbold yelled for the other hangers-on to keep their distance.

The crowd outside heard the girl say, 'Don't murder me, Harry, in my sins!' After that a gunshot rang out in the evening air. He had killed her, and then he coolly stepped outside and walked away into the night, with blood visible on his hand in the light of the doorway, as witnesses later said. He was a man on the edge of reason, and he knew that the only thing left was to end his life, but he claimed later at the trial that his weapon had malfunctioned when he tried to shoot himself in the head. In desperation, he walked to the nearest police officer and confessed.

The sugar daddy in the dock at Lincoln listened while the tales of his lavish spending on the young woman were related. He had treated her very well, and he had snapped when she turned out to be a bitter disappointment to him. There was a feeble attempt at claiming manslaughter, but on flimsy material. He was charged with murder and his response was that it was right he should die. 'Of course I killed her,' he said, 'and I hope when I die I shall join the girl I shot.'

But before the black cap was on the judge's head, he was asked if he wished to speak. Rumbold then made a strange request: he asked for a supply of cigars enough to last him for his last three weeks of life in Lincoln prison. The judge indulged him and let it happen. He smoked himself into a state of agitation, no doubt, before he walked to the scaffold on 19 December 1893, where James Billington was waiting to stretch his neck.

STRANGLED WITH A HANDKERCHIEF, 1903

Leonard Patchett, just twenty-six in 1903, married a woman who had been married to a man who had taken his own life; he was taking on someone very needy, and she should have had affection and care from him. The result was very different, because Patchett was always a jealous, edgy, bad-tempered man. Sarah was five years older than him, and they settled down to married life with several problems, the worst of which was his drinking.

The couple had a daughter and that event, naturally, had the potential to change things for the better but when Sarah took a job as housekeeper to a man called King living in Spencer Street in Lincoln, matters deteriorated. She had left Leonard to live in at her new job. His temper and his drinking had become too much for her to handle. They spent a final week together at Shirebrook, but nothing was worked out between them, and when she said that they had no future, he vowed to follow and kill her. There was no subtlety in this man, and most of the time his words were fired by alcohol. Patchett took a job as a bricklayer in Gainsborough. He had irrational suspicions that his wife was being unfaithful. He would loiter around the house where she worked and accuse the man and his wife of all kinds of deviant behaviour. His mind invented fantasies and plans. Eventually he decided to end the whole relationship in the quickest way: to kill Sarah.

There was nothing secretive about this. He had been staying with his sister in Gainsborough and one day he took a train to Lincoln. Stopping off at a shop, he bought a new collar and said to the assistant, 'I'm about to do something I've never done before . . . if you buy the *Lincolnshire Echo* you will see!' He had arranged to meet and talk with Sarah about the situation and they met in Boultham Park. They were seen walking in Boultham Lane. To people passing by they would have seemed like the usual courting couple taking a stroll. But in fact Patchett strangled her and left her body on a manure heap. It was found three days after they had taken that walk.

Again, the man could not resist telling the world what he had done. He told two people the day after the killing that he had 'done murder'. He even told a room-mate that he had killed someone. When he was arrested and later in court all he could argue in his defence, in sheer desperation, was that he had an alibi that he was on the train to Gainsborough when the murder took place. It didn't take a genius to prove him wrong; a glance at the railway timetable resolved that. In addition to this, two men had seen him in Boultham Lane at around 8 p.m., which was the time he claimed he was waiting to catch a train in the city. Consequently he was hanged on 28 July 1903. He confessed that he had choked his wife with a handkerchief. Now William Billington, experienced executioner, was waiting to tie something around Patchett's neck.

BRIDE OF THREE DAYS SHOT, 1922

On the floor of the White Horse Hotel in Market Deeping, in September 1922, a young woman lay dead; she was just two months short of her nineteenth birthday. She was Ivy Prentice and her mother, a widow, was soon to marry again. In the hotel she was enjoying some time looking at her

Main Street, Market Deeping. Ivy Prentice was shot dead by Frank Fowler at the White Horse Hotel. (Author's Collection)

wedding presents when Frank Fowler, a 35-year-old farm manager, came in the front door with a double-barrelled shotgun in his hands. He had been drinking in the pub earlier, and had gone out of the back door. He was not exactly organised and normal at the time: wearing a grey suit and unlaced boots suggested a certain purposeful disarray. Anyone observing him would have put two and two together and expected a broodiness and dissatisfaction in him that night: he had been drinking alone and slipped out to get the gun. There was no problem about ascertaining any malice aforethought in this case. Fowler knew exactly who he was gunning for: his murderous thoughts were focused on young Ivy and he shot her in the chest; she fell down by the feet of her mother and their friends.

There was then an incredible act of courage on the part of the girl's mother, Edith D'Arcy, who was manager of the pub. She lunged at the gunman as he was aiming to fire at her again. The gun was pushed to one side and a shot was fired through the window. This all happened in a private room, but the customers in the saloon bar heard the shot and rushed in; in no time the gunman was overhauled and held fast by the crowd. The law, in the shape of Sergeant Bennett, soon arrived. Ivy Prentice was confirmed dead by a doctor not long after.

Why did Frank Fowler murder Edith? He was a family friend, and as the *Lincolnshire, Boston and Spalding Free Press* reported, he had given a 'present of a substantial character on the occasion of a recent wedding in the family'.

Ivy's mother, in spite of the traumatic nature of this horrible event, went ahead with her wedding and married her new man, William Kitchener. It must have been a stressful, uneasy atmosphere in that context but it happened, nevertheless. Following hard on this marriage was the inquest, and Fowler was then charged at Bourne police station. Mrs D'Arcy simply said that she had been showing some presents, all the women standing by the table, when the killer came in. She recalled her other daughter, Gertrude, shouting, 'Bring a light, Ivy has been shot!' They were in semi-darkness, and only when the room was lit did the poor mother see and feel the blood on a chair.

The search for a motive went no further than the obvious: Fowler was jealous of the young woman's husband, George. It almost appears as grand tragedy when his words are recalled, spoken as he was grabbed in the pub, with his victim lying dead a few feet away; he said, like some Shakespearean villain, 'I have had my bloody revenge'. Mrs Prentice could not think of any instance when her daughter might have given Fowler any cause to have such a rankling hatred of her. Fowler's burning rancour was expressed in bizarre ways; some time earlier he had faced George Prentice in a bar and hissed at him; then he had returned, taken his hat off and said, 'How is that for a bloody haircut? I will have my own back on you one day, you bugger!' He had been behaving strangely for some time, and the situation was most likely one of inner resentment turning into self-disgust, and then a desire to remove the object of his 'love' from the world, and to do that in a planned, purposeful way. He might have seemed distracted and not fully mentally in control at times, but he knew exactly what he was doing that night in the White Horse Hotel when he took the girl's life. Everything he did suggests a brooding determination to murder and destroy, to take away a life and ruin another, as he made a widower of the young man he had tormented.

The killer pleaded not guilty at Lincoln Assizes, but there was no defence and no question of any other offence than murder with an intention to kill aforethought. Mr Justice Lush had no doubts that he had to place the black cap on his wig and pronounce a sentence of death. Fowler was hanged at Lincoln prison on 13 December 1922, along with George Robinson, who had cut Frances Pacey's throat at Dorrington. The Fowler murder had been one of the most clear-cut and uncomplicated murders of the post-war years, a time in which violent crime escalated across the country.

LEGLESS MAN REPRIEVED, 1954

Lincoln prison on Greetwell Road, north of the city, has experienced some amazing events in its history, including the stunning escape of Irish premier, Eamon de Valera, in February 1919. But one of the strangest stories is surely

Ernest Bond, the man who found Docherty. (Laura Carter)

the scene in the gaol in November 1954 when John Docherty was told that he would not hang. He was in the condemned cell, awaiting his fate at the hands of the executioner for the murder of his fiancée, Sybil Hoy, in Grantham. What was peculiar about all this was that Docherty had lost both legs as he tried to take his own life on the track in front of a train.

Naturally, in such a case, there would be a sensitive issue at the heart of the death sentence. Although his trial had taken only three minutes before sentence was passed, other factors were to emerge later. In cases of physical deformity, the notion of clemency and common humanity might apply, and a royal pardon be given. The reprieve finally came after the Home Secretary had reviewed the case file. In the end, the point to be debated was how a legless man could be hanged with dignity. In effect, it is the Home Secretary who can choose to exercise the royal prerogative of mercy, on behalf of the Crown.

The circumstances of the murder are that John was engaged to Sybil while they were living in Felling, Durham. Their future should have been bright but, partly because of the unhealthy nature of the area they lived in, John contracted tuberculosis and had to be installed in a sanatorium. He came out and it looked as though he had recovered. However, at that time the prevailing fear and concern about the disease was dominated by the thought that someone with this illness would not really be wise to marry: it could go on through progeny, of course. John unfortunately suffered a relapse and was again hospitalised. The outlook was now sombre and very desperate; time went on and Sybil had other young men paying her attention. John was being left out of her life, and he began to pursue her to the point of obsession and harassment. She tried to 'disappear' and be beyond contact, but he found her in Grantham after doing some detective work to locate her. Sybil was staying in Arnoldfield Flats. On the night of her murder she walked out into the dark with the three-year-old child of her friend, little Kevin. A neighbour heard screams and found Sybil beaten and stabbed to death, even though she was with the little boy. It was a dramatic scene: the push chair was upside down when the neighbour ran to see what was happening.

Docherty was crouching in nearby undergrowth, still with the knife in his hands, and he told the neighbour that he had stabbed her a few times. He then fled. She had, in fact, been stabbed no fewer than nineteen times. It was a frenzied attack by a man who was in a murderous rage of revenge.

HMP Lincoln, Greetwell Road. Built in 1872, it was here that hangman William Marwood practised his trade. (Author's Collection)

Not far off, and a little later, Mr Ernest Bond was working with his colleagues, plate-laying on the railway; they paused when a fast train, going at around 70 mph, rushed past. Seconds after it had gone Ernest saw something on the line, something he thought was a bundle of clothes. It was Docherty, and his legs had been sliced off. He was rushed to Grantham hospital and received all the attention he needed, but by 12 August the police were at his bedside and he was charged with murder. In Grantham Guildhall, after entering in a wheelchair, he was charged and remanded in custody. In Lincoln at the Assizes he had made a full confession, not only to murder but to having attempted suicide. The latter was a crime at the time, and was so until 1961. He pleaded guilty and was scheduled to hang on 23 November. It was just eight days before that appointment with the scaffold that he was told about the reprieve. The file with 'Urgent – Capital Case' had been in front of the Home Secretary, and he had made the decision the tabloids had been clamouring for over the previous weeks.

Back in 1907 some of the decisive factors in such decisions had been described by the then Home Secretary, Herbert Gladstone. He had said, 'The motive, the degree of premeditation or deliberation, the amount of

Grantham Guildhall, where Docherty was arrested and charged with murder. (Lincolnshire Libraries)

provocation, the state of mind of the prisoner, his physical condition, his character and antecedents . . . have to be taken into account in every case.' The judge may have had his own opinion at the time of the sentence, but that could not play a part in the passing of the sentence the criminal law demanded, regardless of the state of the man before him in the dock. Docherty had stated clearly, in explanation, that after Sybil left him, 'I did not want to live any more.' She had returned all kinds of presents he had given her and, of course, she had returned his engagement ring. That would have been the final blow. He had no reason to go on living, and his twisted mind thought that she should not live either.

The other factor, however, and it is a very delicate though practical one, is that the professionals who would have had to deal with Docherty in the execution suite at the prison would have been asked to go through a demeaning experience. The prison officers, the chaplain, the governor and indeed the hangman, would have found the notion of hanging a legless man not only absurd but unethical. As to whether the man was of sound mind at the time of the killing, well, yes, he had planned to murder Sybil. But then his attempted suicide was as planned as the murder, so the whole narrative leading to his discovery on the railway line has a tough relentless logic about it. The man who wanted to die that night in front of a train may well have had the same death wish in the prison, but the mode of exit from his life there was surely entirely different from the suicide he wanted; giving someone else the task was too much. The 'system' could not cope with that responsibility, and the media played a part in the dilemma.

Docherty was not the only reprieve case that year; in 1953 five of the eighteen people sentenced to die were reprieved. As to Docherty's sentence, he was to serve not less than fifteen years. The most relieved man in Lincoln on that day when the waited-for news arrived at HMP Lincoln was surely the governor, William Harding. As for the hangman, he must have been delighted that he had been deprived of the practical problem of how one pinions such a man, and how the 'drop' would be calculated accurately.

If we look for comparisons to this strange tale and the act of taking men to execution who are ill or in some way deficient or unsuitable for facing the experience, perhaps the strongest parallel is a political one, because in Kilmainham Gaol, Dublin, after the Easter rebellion of 1916, James Connolly was taken out to face a firing squad. He was on a stretcher and had been taken from a bed in the Castle Hospital before he was carried into the stone-breaking yard to be despatched to the next world. The comparison only serves to illustrate that, when it comes to trying to understand the nature of capital punishment through modern eyes, there is no point in looking for consistency in the routes by which men and women arrived at their fatal appointments at the hands of the state. The inconsistent and often brutal chronicle of twentieth-century capital punishment will always be found to have dozens of stories like this of Docherty: at the centre of these dramas there is always the circumstances of the individual case, and this is invariably at odds with the letter of the law. Not only did questions of insanity raise difficult moral issues in court, but different types of crime caused problems.

Docherty's case illustrates the paradox of a person who wants to end his own life but before this is accomplished the state steps in to decide his fate. Not surprisingly, in this case, the popular media made a sensation of the affair, and in the annals of murder this will always be simply the 'legless man story'. Beneath this, there is a desperately melancholy tale of a man who, like Othello, loved 'not wisely, but too well' and jealousy led to the old formula for the crime of passion: 'If I can't have her, then nobody else will.'

BIBLIOGRAPHY

1. TOM OTTER GIBBETED

Burke, Thomas, *The English Inn*, London, Herbert Jenkins, 1930
Gray, Adrian, *Lincolnshire Tales of Mystery and Murder*, Newbury, Countryside Books, 2004
King, Peter, 'Summary Courts and Social Relations in Eighteenth-Century England', *Past and Present*, no. 183, May 2004
Morgan, Ian, *Tom Otter and the Slaying of Mary Kirkham*, Bakewell, Ashridge Press, 2005
Parish and burial records, South Hykeham and Saxilby

2. MP MURDERED BY UNKNOWN HANDS

Gouldings Household Almanac, Papers of Revd E.H. Jackson
Hill, Sir Francis, *Georgian Lincoln*, Cambridge, Cambridge University Press, 1966
Olney, R.J., *Lincolnshire Politics, 1832–85*, Oxford, Oxford University Press, 1973
Trott, M., 'Political Assassination in Lincoln?', *Lincolnshire Past and Present*, no. 39, Spring 2000

3. A FRIEND MURDERED FOR MONEY

Annual Register, 1847
Davey, B.J., *Rural Crime in the Eighteenth Century*, Hull, University of Hull Press, 1994
Fisher, H.A., *The History of Kirton in Lindsey*, Stamford, Spiegel Press, 1981
Gray, Adrian, *Crime and Criminals in Victorian Lincolnshire*, Stamford, Paul Watkins, 1983
Hawkins, Sir Henry, *Reminiscences*, London, Nelson, 1904
White, William, *History, Gazetteer and Directory of Lincolnshire*, Sheffield, White, 1856
Lincoln, Rutland and Stamford Mercury, 24 December 1847
Lincolnshire Chronicle, 19 December 1847; 4 August 1848
Lincolnshire County Council folder, Convicts of Lincolnshire, 1988
Private correspondence from Stephen Hill
Scunthorpe Evening Telegraph, 31 March 1954

4. The Last Public Execution in the County

Gittings, Robert, *The Older Hardy*, London, Penguin, 1978
Gray, Adrian, *Lincolnshire Murders*, Newbury, Countryside Books, 2004
Tales from the Gallows, Lincolnshire Echo Special Publication, 2001
The Times, 29 July 1859

5. Poisoned by Priscilla and Mary?

Abbott, Geoffrey, *Lipstick on the Noose: Martyrs, Murderers and Mad-women*, Chichester, Summersdale, 2003
Evans, Stewart P., *Executioner: The Chronicles of James Berry*, Stroud, Sutton, 2004
Huggett, Renee, and Berry, Paul, *Daughters of Cain*, London, Allen and Unwin, 1956
Lincolnshire Gazette, 31 October 1868; 26 May 1884
The Times, 29 December 1868
Ward's Historical Guide to Lincoln, 1880
Watson, Katherine, *Poisoned Lives*, London, Hambledon, 2004
Wilson, Patrick, *Murderess*, London, Michael Joseph, 1971

6. Parish Constable Murdered

Blades, Pat, *Hemingby Ancient and Modern: A Village History*, Canwick, Firs, 1996
Davey, B.J., *Lawless and Immoral: Policing a Country Town*, Leicester, Leicester University Press, 1983
Dell, Simon, *The Victorian Policeman*, Shire, Princes Risborough, 2004
Dew, Paul, 'Some Gallant Victorian Policeman', *Journal of the Police History Society*, no. 20, 2005, p. 12
Emsley, Clive, *The English Police*, Harlow, Pearson, 1991
First Report of the Commissioners Appointed to Inquire as to the Best Means of Establishing an Efficient Constabulary Force in England and Wales, 1839 www.murderfiles.com
Fitzgerald, M. et al., *Crime and Society: Readings in History and Theory*, London, Routledge, 1981
Lincolnshire Archives: 3TP1/1 to ¼
The Ultimate Price: The Unlawful Killing of British Police Officers, 1700–1899, CD
Walter, J. Conroy, *Records of the Parish of Horncastle*, Horncastle, Morton, 1904
Wood, Anthony, 'The Municipal Corporations Act, 1835' in *Nineteenth-century Britain*, London, Longman, 1982, pp. 87–9

Woodley, Len, 'The Last Parish Constable to be Murdered', *Journal of the Police History Society*, no. 7 (1992), pp. 47–9

7. THE WIFE KILLER

Clarke, M., 'Some Aspects of Crime and Punishment in Lincolnshire, 1830–50', unpublished thesis, Bishop Grosseteste College, 1979

Harris, Ruth, *Murder and Madness: Medicine, Courts and Society in the Fin de Siècle*, Oxford, Oxford University Press, 1989

Harrison, Brian, *Drink and the Victorians*, Keele, Keele University Press, 1994

Lincolnshire Chronicle, 27 July 1897

Lincolnshire Gazette, August 2004

Phillips, Godfrey, *Outlines of Criminal Law*, Cambridge, Cambridge University Press, 1936

Report of the Committee on Insanity and Crime, London, HMSO, 1924

Wiener, Martin J., 'Judges v. Jurors: Courtroom Tensions in Murder Trials and the Law of Criminal Responsibility in Nineteenth-century England', *History Cooperative*, Fall 1999

8. A CRIME OF PASSION

Lincolnshire Chronicle, 2, 8 November 1918

Lincolnshire Gazette, July 2004

Merskey, Harold, 'Shell Shock', in G. Berrios and H. Freeman (eds), *150 Years of British Psychiatry, 1841–1991*, London, Gaskell, 1991, pp. 245–67

Power, D.J., *Crime, Law and Psychiatry*, Routledge, London, 1979

Stallworthy, John, *Wilfred Owen*, Oxford, Oxford University Press, 1974

Stevenson, David, *1914–1918: The History of the First World War*, London, Penguin, 2005

The Times, 9 November 1918

Van Emden, Richard, and Humphries, Steve, *All Quiet on the Home Front*, London, Headline, 2003

9. FARMHOUSE SHOOTINGS: TEENAGER AND DOG?

Gardner, Alex, *Law Lyrics*, self-published, London, 1897

Gray, Adrian, *Lincolnshire Tales of Mystery and Murder*, Newbury, Countryside Books, 2004

Hastings, Macdonald, *The Other Mr Churchill: A Lifetime of Shooting and Murder*, London, Four Square, 1996

Rawnsley, W.J., *Highways and Byways of Lincolnshire*, London, Macmillan, 1926

Spalding Guardian, special issue, *Crimes of the Century*, 7 June 1991

Lincolnshire Echo, special publication, *Tales from the Gallows*, 27 February 2001
The Times, 2 February 1844; 8 October 1931; 2, 4 January 1932

10. MURDER IN THE FAMILY

ASSI 13/64 XC3601 CL Testimony of Lawrence Oswald Major, pp. 1–8
ASSI 13/64 XC3601 CL Statement by Ethel Major, 3 July 1934
Ballinger, Annette, *Dead Women Walking: Executed Women in English Gaols*, Aldershot, Ashgate, 2000
Canwell, Diane, *Women Who Shocked the Nation*, Derby, Breedon Books, 2002
Daily Express, 2 November 1934
Fryer, Bert, *Recollections of a Country Copper*, Spalding, Fryer, 1996
Hale, Leslie, *Hanged in Error*, London, Penguin, 1961
Huggett, Renee and Berry, Paul, *Daughters of Cain*, London, Allen & Unwin, 1956
Hull Daily Mail, 19 December 1934
Hyde, H. Montgomery, *Norman Birkett*, London, Hamish Hamilton, 1964
Nicholson, D. and Bibbings, Lois, *Feminist Perspectives on Criminal Law*, London, Cavendish, 2000
Royal Commission on Capital Punishment 1949–53, London, HMSO, 1953
The Times, 31 October 1934; 20 December 1934

11. ATTACK IN THE KITCHEN

Home Office Report of the Departmental Committee on Detective Work and Procedure, London, HMSO, 1938
Scunthorpe Evening Telegraph, 24, 25, 26, 27, 28, 29 September; 1, 2, 3, 23, 24 October; 5, 6 November 1945

12. WHO KILLED THE BARTON RECLUSE?

Alert police magazine (internet subscribers only)
Interviews by the author with Constable John Olsson and DS Mick Alcock.
MS letter from Harry Johnson
Scunthorpe Evening Telegraph, 10, 19 April; 2, 4, 5, 6 May 1969

13. A MISCELLANY

Annual Register 1831, pp. 51–2 Chronicle

Boyce, Douglas et al., *Tudor Market Rasen*, Hull, Market Rasen WEA Branch, 1985

Crook, G.T. (ed.), *The Complete Newgate Calendar*, vol. 3, London, Navarre Society, 1926

Essell Collection, Lincoln Central Library

A Full and Particular Account of William Taylor, Executed at The New Drop Lincoln, 1833, Lincoln, Leary, 1833

'The Hearty Repentance of Francis Cartwright', *Lincolnshire Historian*, vol. 2, no. 10, 1983, pp. 30–3

Ketteringham, John R., *A Cathedral Miscellany*, Lincoln, Elpeeko, 1995

Lincolnshire Gazette, November 2004, March 2005

MS. 118600 chapbook, *The Papist Murder*, London, Larkin, 1683, Lincoln Central Library

Spalding Guardian, 7 June 1991

FURTHER READING

Anon., *The Old Bailey Experience*, London, James Fraser, 1833

Busby, Sian, *The Cruel Mother, a Family Ghost Laid to Rest*, London, Short Books, 2004

Christoph, J.B., *Capital Punishment and British Politics*, London, Allen and Unwin, 1962

Cyriax, Oliver, *The Penguin Encyclopaedia of Crime*, London, Penguin, 1996

Deans, R. Storry, *Notable Trials: Romances of the Law Courts*, London, Cassell, 1906

Ellis, John, *Diary of a Hangman*, Glasgow, True Crime Library, 1997

Friar, Stephen, *The Sutton Companion to Local History*, Stroud, Sutton, 2004

Gaute, J.H.H. and Odell, Robin, *The Murderers' Who's Who*, London, Pan, 1979

Harrison, J.F.C., *Early Victorian Britain*, London, Fontana, 1988

Horn, Pamela, *Labouring Life in the Victorian Countryside*, Stroud, Sutton, 1987

Jackson, Robert, *The Chief: The Biography of Gordon Hewart, Lord Chief Justice of England, 1922–1940*, London, Harrap, 1959

Lane, Brian, *The Encyclopaedia of Forensic Science*, London, Headline, 1992

Neild, Basil, *Farewell to the Assizes: The Sixty-one Towns*, Oxford, Garnestone, 1972

Porter, Roy, *Madness: A Brief History*, Oxford, Oxford University Press, 2002

Putwain, David and Sammons, Aidan, *Psychology and Crime*, London, Routledge, 2002

Rees, Sian, *The Floating Brothel*, London, Review, 2001

Stallion, Martin and Wall, David S., *The British Police, Police Forces and Chief Officers, 1829–2000*, Hook, Police History Society, 1999

Taylor, Bernard and Knight, Stephen, *Perfect Murder: A Century of Unsolved Homicides*, London, Grafton, 1988

Tibballs, Geoff, *The Murder Guide to Great Britain*, London, Boxtree, 1994

Tobias, J.J., *Crime and Industrial Society in the Nineteenth Century*, London, Penguin, 1967

Walker, Nigel, *Crime and Insanity in England*, Vol. 1: *The Historical Perspective*, Edinburgh, Edinburgh University Press, 1968

Ward, Jenny, *Crime Busting: Breakthroughs in Forensic Science*, London, Blandford, 1998

Watson, Katherine, *Poisoned Lives: English Poisoners and their Victims*, London, Hambledon, 2000

Wiener, Martin J., *Reconstructing the Criminal: Culture, Law and Policy in England, 1830–1914*, Cambridge, Cambridge University Press, 1990